NEW DIRECTIONS FOR YOUTH DEVELOPMENT

Theory
Practice
Research

2011

Innovations in Child and Youth Programming

A Special Issue from the National AfterSchool Association

Vincent D. LaFontan
Alycia G. Orcena

issue
editors

Gil G. Noam
Editor-in-Chief

JOSSEY-BASS™
An Imprint of
🌀WILEY

INNOVATIONS IN CHILD AND YOUTH PROGRAMMING: A SPECIAL ISSUE FROM THE NATIONAL AFTERSCHOOL ASSOCIATION
Vincent D. LaFontan, Alycia G. Orcena (eds.)
New Directions for Youth Development, Supplement, 2011
Gil G. Noam, Editor-in-Chief
This is a peer-reviewed journal.

Microfilm copies of issues and articles are available in 16mm and 35mm, as well as microfiche in 105mm, through University Microfilms Inc., 300 North Zeeb Road, Ann Arbor, MI 48106-1346.

New Directions for Youth Development is indexed in Academic Search (EBSCO), Academic Search Premier (EBSCO), Contents Pages in Education (T&F), Current Abstracts (EBSCO), Educational Research Abstracts Online (T&F), EMBASE/Excerpta Medica (Elsevier), ERIC Database (Education Resources Information Center), Index Medicus/MEDLINE/PubMed (NLM), MEDLINE/PubMed (NLM), SocINDEX (EBSCO), Sociology of Education Abstracts (T&F), and Studies on Women & Gender Abstracts (T&F).

NEW DIRECTIONS FOR YOUTH DEVELOPMENT (ISSN 1533-8916, electronic ISSN 1537-5781) is part of the Jossey-Bass Psychology Series and is published quarterly by Wiley Subscription Services, Inc., A Wiley Company, at Jossey-Bass, One Montgomery Street, Suite 1200, San Francisco, CA 94104-4594. POSTMASTER: Send address changes to New Directions for Youth Development, Jossey-Bass, One Montgomery Street, Suite 1200, San Francisco, CA 94104-4594.

SUBSCRIPTIONS for individuals cost $89.00 for U.S./Canada/Mexico; $113.00 international. For institutions, agencies, and libraries, $281.00 U.S.; $321.00 Canada/Mexico; $355.00 international. Prices subject to change. Refer to the order form that appears at the back of most volumes of this journal.

EDITORIAL CORRESPONDENCE should be sent to the Editor-in-Chief, Dr. Gil G. Noam, McLean Hospital, Harvard Medical School, 115 Mill Street, Belmont, MA 02478.

Cover photograph by © Christopher Futcher/iStockphoto

www.josseybass.com

Contents

In Pursuit of Excellence

THE NATIONAL AFTERSCHOOL ASSOCIATION (NAA) is committed to a pursuit of excellence in all of its endeavors and contributions in the field, especially those that provide support and services to our members. As part of that quest, NAA has teamed with the Program in Education, Afterschool and Resiliency (PEAR) at Harvard University and Wiley/Jossey-Bass publishers to prepare and produce this special issue of *New Directions for Youth Development*.

In this issue, we are pleased to expand on the excellence of theory, thought, and practice that presenters regularly share at our annual national convention, the outstanding professional development experience of its kind in the field. This peer-reviewed collection of articles on research and best practices is intended to add a deeper and longer-lasting dimension to the professional development experience than might occur at our national convention.

Not everyone is able to attend a national convention. But as we pursue excellence in our work, we must acknowledge that the capacity of each individual cumulatively affects the culture, environment, and success of every after-school program. NAA strives to increase the standards of learning, set high expectations, and lead the search for new knowledge that can be applied to increase the quality of our programming, processes, systems, and practice. This publication is a means to that end.

I hope that you will find each article that follows to be informative, intriguing, and inspiring. Ultimately my hope is that you will find new insights that you can use in your work to help you achieve your goals. I challenge you to join NAA in our efforts to help all after-school professionals expand their views and deepen their understanding of the issues that affect children and youth after school. Together we can achieve excellence for them.

Paul G. Young
President and CEO, National AfterSchool Association

Issue Editors' Notes

THE NATIONAL AFTERSCHOOL ASSOCIATION (NAA) is the leading voice of the after-school profession dedicated to the development, education, and care of children and youth during their nonschool hours. The after-school field has a rich and interesting history of service to children and youth that includes a continuous evolution to define purpose in terms of quality, care, play, protection, intervention, enrichment, socialization, acculturation, and remediation. The diversity of sponsorship, voluntary nature of participation, and unique needs within communities have enabled after-school programs to be child and youth centered, responsive, and independent of the limitations of other institutions. The struggles for identity and emergence of after-school as a complementary development setting connected with schools have shaped and defined the profession and NAA.

Preparing youth for success in tomorrow's workforce is of increasing concern to our nation's schools, communities, policymakers, and businesses. After-school programs are uniquely situated to help. These programs have proven to help youth develop the skills, from leadership to communications to critical thinking, that are needed in the twenty-first-century workplace. The after-school setting provides additional time for learning and uses engaging instructional methods such as project-based learning, real-world application, and smaller group sizes.[1]

The after-school hours

More than 15 million school-age children (26 percent) in the United States are on their own after the school day ends. Among them are more than 1 million children in grades K through 5.[2] Only 8.4 million children (15 percent) participate in after-school programs. An additional 18.5 million would participate if a quality program were available in their community.[3] When school-age children can be involved in quality after-school programming, it reduces the opportunities for juvenile crimes, both as perpetrators and victims. The hours between 3:00 p.m. and 6:00 p.m. are the peak hours for juvenile crime and experimentation with drugs, alcohol, cigarettes, and sex.[4]

Benefits of after-school programs to children, youth, families, and communities

An analysis of seventy-three studies concluded that after-school programs using evidence-based approaches were consistently successful in producing multiple benefits for youth, including improvements in children's personal, social, and academic skills, as well as their self-esteem.[5] The Promising Afterschool Programs Study found that regular participation in high-quality after-school programs is linked to significant gains in standardized test scores and work habits, as well as reductions in behavior problems among disadvantaged students.[6] Middle grade students in New York City programs that were supported by the After-School Corporation improved their math scores and regular school day attendance in high school compared to nonparticipants. High school participants passed more Regents exams and earned more high school credits than nonparticipants did.[7]

National AfterSchool Association

The National School Age Child Care Alliance, now known as NAA, was incorporated as a nonprofit organization in Delaware in 1987. The association emerged from the National Association for the Education of Young Children when leaders began gathering to address unique issues for professionals working with school-age children during out-of-school hours.

NAA is the membership association for professionals who work with children and youth in diverse school and community-based settings to provide a wide variety of extended learning opportunities and care during out-of-school hours. Members include after-school program directors, coordinators, sponsors, frontline staff, school leaders, principals, teachers, paraprofessionals, board of education members, nonprofit leaders, advocates, community leaders, policymakers, researchers, and many others. We respect and celebrate our diversity. NAA is working to ensure that the vision of high-quality learning experiences for all children and youth both in and out of school becomes a reality. NAA recognizes that quality after-school programs provide positive child and youth development and meet a critical need for keeping young people safe and families productively employed. NAA understands that families need a wide range of interesting and age-appropriate programming choices to be available and accessible when their children are not in school.

NAA has held an annual convention for after-school professionals for almost twenty-five years. It declared 2011 to be the Year of Science, with its members working closely with the Afterschool Alliance and the National Summer Learning Association to increase awareness of science, technology, engineering, and math (STEM) learning during out-of-school hours and inspire young learners to become innovators who pursue STEM-related careers. The 2011 conference included a wide variety of professional development opportunities on these topics, as well as physical fitness, program quality improvement, best practices, and staff development.

NAA publishes *AfterSchool Today*, a quarterly magazine dedicated to supporting NAA members of all levels, from those who work one-on-one with students to those in charge of overseeing their program. *AfterSchool Today* is a reflection of the after-school profession. We know the studies on what children would be doing without after-school programs and the statistical research on increase use of alcohol and drugs, sexual experimentation, and delinquent behaviors. *AfterSchool Today* covers topics in a variety of areas:

- "Voice in the Field" a question-and-answer interview with an after-school professional in each issue
- "Program Profile," which examines a specific after-school program
- "True Stories," which focuses on the lives of after-school professionals
- "Great Resources," which describes books and other resources for the after-school field
- Research-based articles on varied topics, including sustainability, health and well-being, teaching methods, evaluations and assessments, professional development, middle school and high school programs, youth development, and program development

About this special issue

The articles we have chosen for this special issue of *New Directions for Youth Development* follow our convention themes closely. Many of the authors have presented at one of our annual conventions, and their sessions were well received and recommended for after-school professionals. We approached these workshop presenters to write articles for this journal based on their research.

The seven articles in this issue encompass both after-school professionals and the after-school environment. The issue opens with a look at school dropout prevention programs as they relate to arts-based community after-school programs. Linda Charmaraman and Georgia Hall present a review of research and discuss why and how arts-based community and out-of-school-time programs can support middle and high school student retention and engagement in school. The second article, by Alexis Menten, focuses on how global learning, the act of teaching school-age children to be globally competent, both during and after school can help advance academic achievement, social and emotional development, and civic engagement, providing young people with the critical knowledge and skills they need to succeed in today's interconnected world.

The third article, by Mat D. Duerden and Ann Gillard, takes a look at how theory-based programming can be a powerful facilitator of positive youth development and provides a model to make it happen. Julianne Gassman and Michael C. Gleason next discuss the mentoring of youth workers. Mentoring is an important method used in the development of others, and the development of youth workers is vitally important to the success of youth programs. The focus of this study, explored in the fourth article, is on the mentoring relationships developed among youth workers and the impact of those relationships on personal development as well as on the advancement of youth programs as a whole.

The fifth article, by Robert L. Fischer, Monica A. G. Craven, and Patricia Heilbron, is based on an evaluation of a fellowship program and the benefits of providing support and professional development for those who work with youth during nonschool hours and connecting after-school programming to education systems; it also takes an ability to understand and navigate complex education systems. We close this issue with Nancy E. Peter's study of youth sports activities and their effects on parents including their personal feelings and behavior both on and off the field.

We hope that you enjoy reading and studying this journal as much as we have enjoyed gathering, reviewing, and editing these articles.

Vincent D. LaFontan
Alycia G. Orcena
Editors

NEW DIRECTIONS FOR YOUTH DEVELOPMENT • DOI: 10.1002/yd

Notes

1. Afterschool Alert Issue Brief, No. 25. (n.d.). Retrieved from http://www.afterschoolalliance.org/researchIssueBriefs.cfm.

2. Afterschool Issue Overview. (n.d.). Retrieved from http://www.afterschoolalliance.org/documents/factsResearch/Fact_Sheet_Afterschool_Essential.pdf.

3. Afterschool Issue Overview. (n.d.)

4. Afterschool Issue Overview. (n.d.)

5. Afterschool Issue Overview. (n.d.)

6. Afterschool Issue Overview. (n.d.)

7. Afterschool Issue Overview. (n.d).

VINCENT D. LAFONTAN *is the director of Farmington Extended Care & Learning, a part of the Farmington Public Schools in Farmington, Connecticut.*

ALYCIA G. ORCENA *is Afterschool and Step Up To Quality coordinator at Ohio Child Care Resource & Referral Association in Columbus, Ohio.*

School dropout prevention: What arts-based community and out-of-school-time programs can contribute

Linda Charmaraman, Georgia Hall

Abstract

Out-of-school-time programs, especially arts-based programs, can be critical players in a community's efforts to prevent school dropout. This research review suggests the following approaches for arts-based programs: (1) recruitment and retention of target populations with multiple risk factors; (2) long-term skill development that engages youth behaviorally, emotionally, and academically rather than a drop-in culture; (3) an emphasis on the critical ingredient of real-world applications through performance; (4) staff development and mentoring; (5) a strategic community-level plan for dropout prevention; (6) and program content reframed toward competencies that underlie better school performance and prosocial behavior, such as communication, initiative, problem solving, motivation, and self-efficacy.

CONCERNS OVER WEAK national academic progress and the growing achievement gap have affirmed that "schools alone are not enough" and have fueled interest in understanding the potential role that community-based and out-of-school-time (OST) programs can play in retaining middle and high school youth in

Support and guidance for this article were provided by the West Michigan Center for Arts and Technology.

NEW DIRECTIONS FOR YOUTH DEVELOPMENT, SUPPLEMENT 2011 © WILEY PERIODICALS, INC.
Published online in Wiley Online Library (wileyonlinelibrary.com) • DOI: 10.1002/yd.416

9

school.[1] Although there are substantial research findings on traditional education classrooms and systems related to student dropout, much less work has been done to explore dropout prevention as an outcome of community-based and OST programs. The majority of these types of programs incorporate direct academic support in their model to reengage students in their own learning and motivation to graduate. In addition, a number of programs support student learning and engagement using instructional tools that are not traditionally considered academically focused, such as the visual and performing arts. The unique role of community and OST arts-based programs in dropout prevention efforts is explored in this article. Our goal is to inform those working in existing and emerging arts-based community and OST programs and youth workers about how to incorporate effective dropout prevention strategies and practices in their programs.

Three key questions guide this article:

- What are the predictors of high school dropout?
- What are best practices components from community dropout prevention programs?
- What is known about the role of arts in community-based or OST programming as a dropout prevention program element?

Methods

We conducted a review exploring the current discussion and research findings on high school dropout prevention as related to community-based and OST programs, with a specific emphasis on arts-based programs. We used a Web document search and several electronic databases, including Academic Search Complete and PsycInfo, to search for recent journal articles, reports, research briefs, and conference proceedings. The Web site and document search process included reviewing materials from organizations such as the Forum for Youth Investment, National Dropout Prevention Center, U.S. Department of Education, Center for Mental

NEW DIRECTIONS FOR YOUTH DEVELOPMENT • DOI: 10.1002/yd

Health in Schools at UCLA, and Communities in Schools. In total, we selected 105 documents for initial review. This article incorporates information from over 40 of the most relevant selected documents. We primarily focused on literature and research published within the past fifteen years, reviews of the literature, and those who reported on evaluation or research findings that could inform programming and approaches for arts-based programs. For purposes of this article, "arts-based programming" refers to the visual arts (for example, painting, textile arts), performing arts (for example, dance, drama, music), and media arts (for example, digital photography, video-making).

Predicting high school dropout

According to the Center for Research on the Education of Students Placed at Risk, approximately one thousand U.S. high schools have a 50 percent rate of graduation.[2] The long-term cost of school failure includes increased likelihood of being unemployed, committing crimes, receiving public assistance, and being incarcerated.[3] Dropouts are less likely to receive health insurance and have pension plans, be in good health, and live as long as those who graduated.[4] In 2007, the National Dropout Prevention Center and Communities in Schools conducted a comprehensive literature review with the goal of identifying risk factors or conditions that significantly increase high school dropout rates.[5] In general, their findings pointed to a multitude of dropout risk factors in several domains: individual, family, school, and community.

No single risk factor can accurately predict who is at risk for school failure, but risks increase when several factors are considered together. Dropouts are not a homogeneous population, and many times a lengthy process of disengagement, which begins before kindergarten, leads to the process of dropping out. In other words, it is not a single event that leads to dropping out but a process of risk factors that build and compound over time. Although most dropouts leave school by eleventh or twelfth grade, two studies have identified earlier patterns of dropout: tenth grade in Chicago and Baltimore and ninth grade in Philadelphia.[6]

One of the most critical time periods for students when they begin to show warning signals is in the transition to middle and then to high school—respectively, sixth and ninth grades—even in the first month of the school year.[7] In addition to having to negotiate a new and often larger institutional setting, students find that the course work has become more intellectually demanding, teachers are less supportive, peer groups are larger, relationships are more complicated, and temptations become greater at the same time that they begin to experience more personal freedom.[8] The following sections provide a brief overview of the most significant contributors to dropout during the middle or high school years.

Early adult responsibilities

When children are forced to take on adult responsibilities, there is an increased likelihood of falling behind in school and eventually dropping out. Such responsibilities include taking on a job to help pay for family expenses, taking care of siblings, or becoming a teen parent.[9]

Social attitudes, values, and behavior

Antisocial behavior in the early adolescent years, such as substance abuse, early sexual risk taking, and violence, has been linked to dropping out of school.[10] How adolescents spend their free time also plays a role; for example, teens who do not read for pleasure each week are more likely to drop out.[11]

School performance

Whether it is measured by course failure, grades, or test scores, academic performance is one of the strongest predictors of dropout starting even in the first grade through the elementary school years into middle school and eventually into high school.[12]

NEW DIRECTIONS FOR YOUTH DEVELOPMENT • DOI: 10.1002/yd

School engagement and disengagement

Students who become detached from their academic studies typically start to demonstrate patterns of absenteeism and cutting class, not completing homework on a regular basis, and coming to class unprepared.[13] When students indicate low educational expectations, such as being uncertain about graduating from high school or not having any plans beyond high school, they are at risk for dropping out before getting a diploma.[14] The psychological reasons given for dropping out of school include a lack of a sense of belonging at school, not feeling connected to any teachers, or a generalized dislike of school.[15] Dropouts tend to associate themselves with friends who are also at risk of school failure.[16] One major sign of social disengagement is lack of involvement in school-based extracurricular activities, such as sports, school newspaper, and clubs.[17]

Family background characteristics

Above all other family characteristics, socioeconomic status appears to be the most consistent factor that affects dropout, whether measured through parent education level, occupation, or income.[18] Those youth at most risk of school failure are students from nontraditional homes, such as non-English-speaking households and single-parent or stepparent families.[19] Family conflict, health problems, residential moves, and other family crises such as divorce, remarriage, or death all have a negative impact on the likelihood that a young person will stay in school.[20] Male students from minority backgrounds are particularly at risk for dropping out.[21] Latino and African American boys are much more likely to repeat a grade level than white boys or girls of any racial/ethnic group. Boys, in particular minority boys, are suspended or expelled from school in higher numbers than girls are.[22]

Family engagement and commitment to education

Low parental expectations about school, parents who dropped out when they were young, or siblings who have dropped out place students at high risk to drop out themselves.[23] Parents' actions regarding the importance of education send implicit messages to their children, for instance, avoiding talk about academic performance or behavior, rarely getting involved in PTA types of activities, and a lack of study aids and homework monitoring in the home.[24]

OST dropout prevention efforts

Given the risk factors reviewed, many of which highlight the critical gap in caring adults who can offer guidance and help young people thrive, as well as the perils of unstructured time alone, OST programs can be critical players in a community's efforts to prevent school dropout. However, many dropout prevention programs are being used throughout the country with almost no documentation of their development or little or no long-term follow-up data to determine impacts on youth over time.[25] Positive youth outcomes are more likely to occur when a program's theoretical rationale, objectives, goals, and outcome evaluation data have been carefully reviewed.

Starting from a list of evidence-based programs compiled by Sharon Mihalic at the Center for the Study and Prevention of Violence and cross-referencing the listed programs with other sources, the National Dropout Prevention Center identified fifty exemplary programs.[26] These programs met the criteria of being ranked in the top tier by at least two sources; were currently in operation; had consistent, positive outcomes; targeted students from kindergarten through twelfth grade; and had no major recent revisions to their program. One of the programs showing at least moderate to large effects on positive school behaviors is Talent Search, which operates in Texas and Florida and serves over nine thousand eight hundred mainly low-income students who are future first-generation college students. The Talent Search curriculum has three parts:

• Individualized academic assistance for their current school work, such as tutoring and counseling

- Exploration of future careers and colleges, including aptitude assessment, visits to college campuses, and preparation for college entrance exams
- Workshops for participants' families

Another program that has demonstrated positive effects on school behaviors, Quantum Opportunity, emphasizes long-term commitment and case management follow-up over several years to lower dropout rates and track success. Operating across several states, including Ohio, Texas, Tennessee, Pennsylvania, and Washington, along with Washington, D.C., this program combines mentoring, tutoring, recreational programs, and financial incentives to attract at-risk youth to their programs and retain them.

Of the top fifty evidence-based dropout programs identified by Mihalic,[27] the most frequently used strategy of life skills development (which was incorporated into two-thirds of these programs) entailed developing the following:

- Communication skills
- Healthy relationships
- Problem-solving and decision-making skills
- Critical thinking
- Assertiveness
- Peer resistance and selection
- Stress reduction
- Leadership
- Appreciation for diversity

The second most frequently used strategy was family strengthening activities, such as providing specific training to parents on how to assist their child academically. About half of the top fifty programs included parents as a critical part of their dropout prevention framework. The third most frequent strategy was academic support, such as homework assistance and tutoring, which about one-quarter of the evidence-based programs used.

Although the primary goals of each of these dropout programs are focused on positive school engagement and academic skill building, the application of these goals is centered not only around direct academic support but also on developing the intermediary skills that are critical to academic success, such as developing positive relationships with others, learning how to communicate effectively, and appreciating diversity. These types of skills are critical for nurturing young people who need a positive and supportive environment to bring their assets to the foreground and become productive citizens.

Arts-based youth development

In resource-poor communities, young people may have a particularly difficult time finding opportunities to feel valued and accepted as engaged citizens, which makes youth development programs so vital in order for young people to remain connected to their communities.[28] With ongoing national education budget cuts necessitating tangible evidence of learning gains that will improve high-stakes testing results, arts classes fall victim to cuts, leaving a cultural void in the school curriculum.[29] In some communities, arts-based alliances between nonprofit organizations and businesses have formed to fill some of these institutional gaps in order to involve young people in collaborative experiences that increase their knowledge and skills during the OST hours.

The Arts Education Partnership and the President's Committee on the Arts and the Humanities developed Champions of Change: The Impact of the Arts on Learning, an initiative that explored the impact of arts education experiences on young people's lives.[30] They compiled seven research teams that examined a variety of art education programs, both in and out of school, using quantitative and qualitative methodologies. Although the teams conducted their investigations independently, a notable consensus existed among their findings that pertained to theories regarding how and why the arts change the learning experience.

Seven common themes emerged regarding why the arts change the learning experience. They:

1. Reach students who are not being reached through other means
2. Reach students in ways that had not been tapped into before
3. Connect students to themselves and with each other
4. Transform the learning context
5. Provide learning opportunities for the adults in young people's lives
6. Provide different challenges for students who are already considered successful
7. Provide a real-world learning experience

There were also seven common themes regarding how the arts change the learning experience. They:

1. Provide direct access to the arts and artists`
2. Require significant staff training and administrative support
3. Support extended engagement in the ongoing artistic process
4. Encourage self-directed learning
5. Promote complexity and challenges
6. Allow management of risk and vulnerability
7. Engage community leaders and resources

In their list of promising practices from twenty-three organizations using a variety of media arts and technologies, Baker, Jeffers, and Light encourage programs to:

- Focus on the role of participants and adults as facilitators, role models, and co-explorers
- Prepare young people for the workforce by building strong program relationships with business and industry and by exhibiting the work that young people do to potential and current community partners

- Teach technological literacy but also teach skills that are not technology specific, such as self-expression, teamwork skills, and linking technology content with other types of projects
- Maintain a family-like sense of community by developing a sense of work ethics and interpersonal skills
- Give priority to underserved youth, particularly girls, and recruit staff who reflect participants' identities and communities[31]

Out-of-school arts learning outcomes

According to the U.S. Department of Justice, after-school arts programming not only increases the academic achievement of at-risk youth but also decreases drug use and juvenile delinquency, increases self-esteem, and increases positive interactions and connections with peers and adults.[32] Students have attributed these positive outcomes through arts education to increased caring and attention from supportive arts instructors, an increase in self-esteem, and a sense of accomplishment through the learning opportunities.[33] For economically disadvantaged youth, studies have shown that access to arts education benefits low-income populations in unique ways. In an eleven-year national study of youth in low-income neighborhoods, McLaughlin found that those who participated in community-based arts programs were more likely to have high academic achievement, be elected to class office, participate in a math or science fair, or win an award for creative writing.[34] The programs studied included those based on athletics, community service, and arts. Surprisingly, although youth in the arts programs were identified as most at risk, these young people were doing the best compared to youth in the programs based on community service or athletics. McLaughlin hypothesized that the characteristics particular to arts-based program settings and culture make them more effective than the other alternatives.

NEW DIRECTIONS FOR YOUTH DEVELOPMENT • DOI: 10.1002/yd

Recommendations

The research conducted for this article suggests the following dropout prevention program strategies and approaches for arts-based community and OST programs.

Focus on identifying, recruiting, and retaining the target population

A review of program goals and priorities in order to identify a specific target population for recruitment would be worthwhile. Mathematica researchers have concluded that dropout prevention programs typically end up serving students who were not at risk of dropping out and do not serve students who are at risk.[35] In order to avoid this mismatch of service delivery to the appropriate population, program developers might pay attention to the high-risk individual and family characteristics noted previously in this article to identify, target, and recruit purposively for programs. Wright, John, and Sheel recommend a three-stage process for recruiting and sustaining involvement of parents and youth:

1. Community mapping and active recruitment strategies—for example, identifying community characteristics and resources; setting up booths in malls; and posting advertisements at malls, housing projects, schools, community-based organizations, ethnic organizations, and parks and recreation centers
2. Inviting parents to an open house to explain any participant incentives and remove obstacles for participation, such as transportation issues
3. Matching artists and staff members to participant characteristics, such as race/ethnicity[36]

Since transition into high school has been identified as one of the critical periods for dropout prevention, focusing on recruiting at-risk eighth and ninth graders would be an important step. Partnerships with local schools, including key relationships with principals, guidance counselors, and in-school arts and technology teachers, could lead to numerous referrals and opportunities to make classroom presentations, hold school assemblies, and offer information through informal presentations and disseminating program information during school orientations. Current participants in the program can serve as recruiters by spreading the word to their friends and classmates to come check out the program.

To increase retention of students over a longer period of time, programs could provide leadership opportunities for current students to become mentors to younger cohorts and apprentices to adults in real-world jobs and to be given greater levels of decision-making capacities within the program itself. For instance, participants can periodically engage with staff in focus groups to reflect on the program and how to improve it. More committed participants can also be offered a position as assistant to the director, a peer leader, or a youth representative on an advising committee or board.

Offer dynamic arts-based programming that engages youth

It would make sense for programs to review attendance levels of current course offerings, student feedback, and observations of meaningful staff-youth relationships during the program. A broad assessment of current teaching practices and instructional approaches would inform a process of redirecting practice toward a dynamic teaching model that engages youth behaviorally, emotionally, and cognitively. In addition, programs should create opportunities for sustained youth engagement and reflection through ongoing projects, youth journals, and portfolios.

Long-term engagement can be encouraged by sequencing courses in a way that provides continuation incentive. For example, a first course sequence could begin with script-writing, then move on to video production, and then a course on postproduction and editing, all of which require successful completion before taking the next course. Programs might consider emphasizing a performing arts genre, such as spoken word or poetry, drama, dance, or music, in order to foster community dialogue tied to showcase opportunities. In terms of specific curricula, research suggests that programming should not just focus on the delivery of services and activities, but also seek to develop and maintain trusting social relationships with peers and adults. One way to encourage discussion and connection between participants is to start the day with "check-ins" so that the staff members are in touch with how their students are doing at school, home, and life in general. Caring relationships with mentors have been shown to be key to program retention and positive outcomes.

A purposeful plan with multiple strategies to ensure program impact should be in place to address multiple risk factors across the domains of the individual, family, school, and environment.[37] For example, incorporating an element of tutoring or counseling on top of arts program activities might increase graduation rates.

Emphasize performance and recognition

Prior research on arts-based programs emphasizes the critical ingredient of audience and real-world applications through performance. If programs were to adopt a performance aspect to their model, youth workers should pay particular attention to each course being suitable for showcasing or performances such that no student is left out of the performance aspect. Once successful exhibitions have showcased student work with positive feedback from a familiar audience of family, peers, and community members, programs may take the next step to professionalize student work and increase students' confidence and networking opportunities by entering them into arts contests and local, regional, or national youth arts and media arts festivals. In terms of appreciation events and ways to encourage long-term enrollment, programs have incorporated an end-of-year awards ceremony in which every student receives an award for his or her commitment or an individualized award for improving in particular ways, as identified by the staff instructor.

Offer training on youth development to enhance staff mentoring skills

It is critical to recruit staff who reflect participant characteristics in race/ethnicity and gender. Staff instructors should not only be professionals in their fields with connections to industry, but they need to have certain personal characteristics such as interacting and communicating well with at-risk youth; a willingness to mentor youth over time both within the subject taught and outside; an ability to understand the different pathways that young people might need (for example, different learning styles) to grow at their own pace; and a sense of passion for their art, which may be contagious to their students, motivating them to achieve and hone their new craft. Programs can enhance the contribution of master teachers and mentors by including extensive professional development on positive youth development theory and approaches. In addition, programs can support dedicated time for teachers to collaborate on student projects, check in on student progress, and help one another troubleshoot solutions for keeping students engaged in the program itself and at school.

Involve parents and community

Lack of student school engagement is associated with parental lack of school engagement, parental commitment to education, and parental expectations for children. For programs to encourage parent involvement, thereby offering more opportunities for parents to become familiar with their children's talents and interests, the program might invite parents to open houses, exhibitions, fundraisers, and a special parent day at program classes so that students and parents can have the experience of learning and cocreating together. Parents might be invited to speak at these performances and exhibits, reflecting on their reaction to watching the young people perform. Open house events might tie in school engagement topics, such as credits needed to graduate or tutoring and counseling, so that parents and students have opportunities to discuss progress in school in a structured yet informal way.

In addition, a strategic plan for dropout prevention needs to be formulated at the community level. It is critical to work with community partners such as other youth-serving organizations, mental health, social services, and educational institutions to reach consensus, establish priorities, and do action planning around dropout prevention. In order to establish and maintain community ties and contribute to the community's cultural awareness of youth ideas, youth arts projects can be displayed and showcased at community partners' office buildings, health centers, community theaters, museums, or galleries.

Evaluate intermediary skills

Consideration should be given to reframing program planning and content toward skills and competencies that underlie better school performance and prosocial behaviors. Program content, instructional practices, and outcome evaluation should focus on intermediary skills besides the long-term goal of dropout prevention, such as engagement, expectations, relationships with adults, relationships with peers, communication, initiative, problem solving, motivation, self-efficacy, and self-competence. A menu of both quantitative and qualitative measures will offer a full picture of progress on youth outcomes and participation experiences.

Conclusion

The research literature on dropout prevention points to a number of school-based, classroom-based, and district-based strategies that have been demonstrated to support keeping students in school. It appears that the most important activity that community-based and OST programs can do is to work on the components of dropout prevention that can also apply to settings outside the school experience—for example:

- Reengage youth who have become or are in danger of disengaging from school.

- Provide opportunities for attachment and the development of close and caring relationships with an adult.
- Provide opportunities for involvement in an extracurricular endeavor, such as appreciating the arts and learning principles of art design.
- Offer a social and learning environment that is supportive and embraces positive youth development principles.

This article has looked at the connection between two often separate efforts within youth development: dropout prevention and arts-based programming. Such knowledge can inform and guide youth workers and program coordinators in arts-based community and OST programs in developing, implementing, and integrating effective strategies and practices for dropout prevention within their local programs and communities.

Notes

1. Mass Insight Education. (2002). *Schools alone are not enough: How after-school and summer programs help raise student achievement*. Boston, MA: Author.

2. Balfanz, R., & Legters, N. (2004, September). *Locating the dropout crisis* (Tech. Rep. No. 70). Baltimore, MD: Johns Hopkins University, Center for Research on the Education of Students Placed at Risk. Retrieved from http://www.csos.jhu.edu/crespar/techReports/Report70.pdf.

3. Jerald, D. C. (2006). *Identifying potential dropouts: Key lessons for building an early warning data system*. Washington, DC: American Diploma Project Network, Achieve. Retrieved from http://www.achieve.org/files/FINAL-dropouts_0.pdf.

4. Jerald. (2006).

5. Hammond, C., Linton, D., Smink, J., & Drew, S. (2007). *Dropout risk factors and exemplary programs*. Clemson, SC: National Dropout Prevention Center, Communities in Schools.

6. Alexander, K. L., Entwisle, D. R., & Kabbani, N. S. (2001). The dropout process in life course perspective: Early risk factors at home and school. *Teachers College Record, 103*, 760–822; Ensminger, M. E., & Slusarcick, A. L. (1992). Paths to high school graduation or dropout: A longitudinal study of a first-grade cohort. *Sociology of Education, 65*, 95–113.

7. Neild, R. C., & Balfanz, R. (2006). An extreme degree of difficulty: The educational demographics of urban neighborhood high schools. *Journal of Education for Students Placed at Risk, 11*(2), 123–141.

8. Jerald. (2006); McPartland, J. M. (1994). *Exploring the complexity of early dropout causal structures*. Baltimore, MD: Johns Hopkins University.

9. Jordan, W. J., Lara, J., & McPartland, J. M. (1994). *Exploring the complexity of early dropout causal structures.* Baltimore, MD: Johns Hopkins University; Rosenthal, B. S. (1998). Nonschool correlates of dropout: An integrative review of the literature. *Children and Youth Services Review, 20*(5), 413–433; Cairns, R. B., Cairns, B. D., & Neckerman, H. J. (1989). Early school dropout: Configurations and determinants. *Child Development, 60,* 1437–1452; Gleason, P., & Dynarski, M. (2002). How can we help? What we have learned from recent federal dropout prevention evaluations. *Journal of Education for Students Placed at Risk, 7,* 43–69. Rumberger, R. W. (2001). *Why students drop out of school and what can be done.* Paper prepared for the conference Dropouts in America: How Severe Is the Problem? What Do We Know About Intervention and Prevention? Cambridge, MA.

10. Battin–Pearson, S., & Newcomb, M. D. (2000). Predictors of early high school dropout: A test of five theories. *Journal of Educational Psychology, 92,* 568–582; Ekstrom, R. B., Goertz, M. E., Pollack, J. E., & Rock, D. A. (1986). Who drops out of high school and why? Findings from a national study. *Teachers College Record, 87,* 356–373; Wehlage, G. G., & Rutter, R. A. (1986). Dropping out: How much do schools contribute to the problem? *Teachers College Record, 87,* 374–392.

11. Gleason & Dynarski. (2002).

12. Alexander et al. (2001); Lloyd, D. N. (1978). Prediction of school failure from third-grade data. *Educational and Psychological Measurement, 38*(4), 1193–1200; Battin–Pearson & Newcomb. (2000); Ingels, S. J., Curtin, T. R., Kaufman, P., Alt, M. N., & Chen, X. (2002). *Coming of age in the 1990s: The eighth grade class of 1988 12 years later* (NCES 2002–321). Washington, DC: National Center for Education Statistics, U.S. Department of Education; Ekstrom et al. (1986); Elliott, D. S., & Voss, H. L. (1974). *Delinquency and dropout.* Lanham, MD: Lexington Books; Gleason & Dynarski. (2002).

13. Ekstrom et al. (1986); Kaufman, P., Bradbury, D., & Owings, J. (1992). *Characteristics of at-risk students in the NELS: 88.* Washington, DC: National Center for Education Statistics, Office of Educational Research and Improvement, U.S. Department of Education; Wehlage & Rutter. (1986).

14. Alexander, K. L., Entwisle, D. R., & Horsey, C. S. (1997). From first grade forward: Early foundations of high school dropout. *Sociology of Education, 70,* 87–107. Gleason & Dynarski. (2002); Rumberger. (2001).

15. Ekstrom et al. (1986); Jordan et al. (1994).

16. Cairns et al. (1989).

17. Elliott & Voss. (1974); Ingels et al. (2002).

18. Alexander et al. (2001); Battin–Pearson & Newcomb. (2000); Cairns et al. (1989); Lehr, C. A., Johnson, D. R., Bremer, C. D., Cosio, A., & Thompson, M. (2004, May). *Essential tools: Increasing rates of school completion: Moving from policy and research to practice.* Minneapolis, MN: National Center on Secondary Education and Transition; Rumberger. (2001); Schargel, F. P. (2004). Who drops out and why. In J. Smink & F. P. Schargel (Eds.), *Helping students graduate: A strategic approach to dropout prevention.* Larchmont, NY: Eye on Education; Wehlage & Rutter. (1986).

19. Rosenthal. (1998); Rumberger. (2001).

20. Alexander et al. (1997); Catalano, R., & Hawkins, J. D. (1995). *Communities that care: Risk-focused prevention using the social development strategy.* Seattle, WA: Developmental Research and Programs; Lehr et al. (2004, May); Rosenthal. (1998).

21. Rumberger, R. W. (2004). Why students drop out of school. In G. Orfield (Ed.), *Dropouts in America: Confronting the graduation rate crisis* (pp. 131–155). Cambridge, MA: Harvard Education Press.

22. Mead, S. (2006). *The truth about boys and girls.* Washington, DC: Education Sector. Retrieved from http://www.cpec.ca.gov/CompleteReports /ExternalDocuments/ESO_BoysAndGirls.pdf; American Psychological Association Zero Tolerance Task Force. (2009). Are zero tolerance policies effective in schools? An evidentiary review and recommendation. *American Psychologist, 63,* 852-862.

23. Alexander et al. (2001); Catalano & Hawkins. (1995); Ensminger, M. E., Lamkin, R. P., & Jacobson, N. (1996). School leaving: A longitudinal perspective including neighborhood effects. *Child Development, 67,* 2400–2416; Gleason & Dynarski. (2002); Kaufman et al. (1992).

24. Rumberger. (2004); Ekstrom et al. (1986); Goldschmidt, P., & Wang, J. (1999). When can schools affect dropout behavior? A longitudinal multilevel analysis. *American Educational Research Journal, 36,* 715–738; Jimerson, S., Egeland, B., Sroufe, A., & Carlson, B. (2000). A prospective longitudinal study of high school dropouts examining multiple predictors across development. *Journal of School Psychology, 38,* 525–549; Kaufman et al. (1992); Teachman, J. D., Paasch, K., & Carver, K. (1996). Social capital and dropping out of school early. *Journal of Marriage and the Family, 58,* 773–783.

25. Catalano, R. F., Berglund, M. L., Ryan, J.A.M., Lonczak, H. S., & Hawkins, J. D. (2004). Positive youth development in the United States: Research findings on evaluations of positive youth development programs. *Annals of the American Academy of Political and Social Science, 591,* 98–124; Rumberger. (2001).

26. Mihalic, S. F. (2005). *The matrix of prevention programs.* Boulder: University of Colorado at Boulder, Center for the Study and Prevention of Violence, Institute of Behavioral Science. Retrieved from http://www.colorado.edu /cspv/blueprints/matrixfiles/matrix.pdf; Hammond, C., Linton, D., Smink, J., & Drew, S. (2007). *Dropout risk factors and exemplary programs.* Clemson, SC: National Dropout Prevention Center, Communities in Schools.

27. Mihalic. (2005).

28. Kegler, M., Oman, R. F., Vesely, S., McLeroy, K., Aspy, C. B., Rodine, S., & Marshall, L. (2005). Relationships among youth assets, neighborhood characteristics, and community resources. *Health Education and Behavior, 32*(3), 380–397; Leventhal, T., & Brooks-Gunn, J. (2000). The neighborhoods they live in: The effects of neighborhood residence on child and adolescent outcomes. *Psychological Bulletin, 126*(2), 309–337; Leventhal, T., & Brooks-Gunn, J. (2003). Children and youth in neighborhood contexts. *Current Directions in Psychological Science, 12*(1), 27–31. Swisher, R., & Whitlock, J. (2004). How neighborhoods matter for youth development. In S. F.

Hamilton & M. A. Hamilton (Eds.), *The youth development handbook: Coming of age in American communities* (pp. 216–238). Thousand Oaks, CA: Sage.

29. Ersing, R. L. (2009). Building the capacity of youths through community cultural arts: A positive youth development perspective. *Best Practices in Mental Health, 5*(1), 26–43.

30. Fiske, E. B. (Ed.). *Champions of change: The impact of the arts on learning.* Washington, DC: President's Committee on the Arts and Humanities. Retrieved from http://artsedge.kennedy-center.org/champions/pdfs/ChampsReport.pdf.

31. Baker, T., Jeffers, L., & Light, D. (1999). *Learning to work: Promising practices in youth development and career preparation using technology and media.* New York, NY: EDC/Center for Children and Technology.

32. Clawson, H. J., & Coolbaugh, K. (2001, May). *The YouthArts Development Project.* Retrieved from http://www.ncjrs.gov/pdffiles1/ojjdp/186668.pdf

33. Weitz, J. H. (1996). *Coming up taller: Arts and humanities programs for children and youth at risk.* Washington, DC: President's Committee for the Arts and Humanities. Retrieved from http://www.eric.ed.gov/PDFS/ED410353.pdf.

34. McLaughlin, W. M. (2000). *Community counts: How youth organizations matter for youth development.* Washington, DC: Public Education Network.

35. Gleason & Dynarski. (2002).

36. Wright, R., John, L., & Sheel, J. (2007). Lessons learned from the National Arts and Youth Demonstration Project: Longitudinal study of a Canadian after-school program. *Journal of Child and Family Studies, 16,* 49–59.

37. Hammond et al. (2007).

LINDA CHARMARAMAN *is a research scientist at the National Institute on Out-of-School Time at the Wellesley Centers for Women at Wellesley College in Massachusetts.*

GEORGIA HALL *is a research scientist at the National Institute on Out-of-School Time at the Wellesley Centers for Women at Wellesley College in Massachusetts.*

Expanding horizons through global learning in out-of-school time

Alexis Menten

Abstract

The demands and opportunities of globalization involve not only America's economic competitiveness, but also national security, the need for tolerance in increasingly diverse communities, and a need to solve pressing social issues. To be successful, students need a comprehensive and integrated set of global learning experiences that help them expand their horizons from their neighborhood to the rest of the world. Schools as well as community partners and after-school and summer programs all have an important role to play in restructuring educational opportunities to help all students become globally competent.

IT IS A CLICHÉ that the world is getting smaller. But as rapid economic, technological, and social changes shrink our world, our understanding of it has to grow.[1] At the same time, although we live in an interconnected world, many of America's young people have not had the chance to explore beyond their neighborhoods. Out-of-school-time programs face both an urgent challenge and a new opportunity to continue their innovative work preparing young people for future success.

The demands and opportunities of globalization today involve not only America's economic competitiveness, but also national

Portions of this article are excerpts from two Asia Society publications, which are reprinted with permission: *Expanding horizons: Building global literacy in afterschool programs* (2009) and *Educating for global competence: Preparing our youth to engage the world* (2011).

security, the need for tolerance in increasingly diverse communities, and a need to solve pressing social issues. Knowledge about the rest of the world, skills to communicate and collaborate across boundaries, and a commitment to active and informed citizenship are now critical to success in both the workplace and life in general.[2] To be successful as they grow and mature, students need a comprehensive and integrated set of global learning experiences that help them expand their horizons from their neighborhood to the rest of the world.

Global learning represents a crucial shift in our understanding of the purpose of education in a changing world. Young people everywhere and from all backgrounds deserve the opportunity to access global learning opportunities that help them succeed in the global economy and contribute as global citizens. Schools as well as community partners and after-school and summer programs all have important roles to play in helping youth become globally competent.

Defining global competence

The term *global competence* has emerged as a way to articulate the knowledge and capacities youth need for success in the interconnected world of the twenty-first century. Globally competent students possess the knowledge, skills, and dispositions to understand issues of global significance and act creatively to address them.

Asia Society is a global nonprofit organization that works to strengthen relationships and promote understanding among the people, leaders, and institutions of the United States and Asia across the fields of arts and culture, policy and business, and education. In education, the Asia Society Partnership for Global Learning develops youth to be globally competent citizens, workers, and leaders by equipping them with the knowledge and skills needed for success in an increasingly interconnected world. In 2010, Asia Society chaired the Global Competence Taskforce convened by the Council of Chief State School Officers that brought together representatives from leading universities, nonprofit organizations, and state education agencies across the United States.[3] The resulting book, *Educating for global competence: Preparing our youth to engage the world*, defines *global competence* as the capacity and disposition to understand and act creatively on issues of global significance. To achieve global competence, all young people must be able to investigate the world of their immediate environment and beyond, recognize their own and others' perspectives, communicate ideas to diverse audiences, and take action to improve conditions both locally and globally.[4] In order to develop high-quality global learning opportunities, educators need to know what each of these aspects of global competence involves and what each component looks like when youth demonstrate it.

Investigate the world

Global competence starts by being aware, curious, and interested in learning about the world. It requires the capacity to pose and explore questions that are relevant personally, locally, nationally, and globally. These are questions that do not necessarily have one right answer, but globally competent students are able to systematically engage them intellectually and emotionally by synthesizing evidence, perspectives, and experiences to draw defensible conclusions.

For example, at a University of Chicago charter school, children wanted to talk about violence and ways to resolve conflict. The after-school staff first helped children connect their own African American roots to Martin Luther King Jr.'s quest for nonviolence in the United States. From there, they learned about Gandhi's nonviolent campaign to liberate India from British rule. Then they worked on strategies for resolving violence in their school community.

Recognize their own and others' perspectives

Globally competent students recognize that they have a particular perspective that others may or may not share. They are able to

identify influences on their own and others' perspectives and articulate the implications of these perspectives on actions. Globally
competent students can compare and contrast their perspectives
with those that others hold and integrate their own and others'
viewpoints to construct a new one when needed.

At a New York City after-school site run by The After-School
Corporation and Good Shepherd Services, eight year olds realized
that water is a finite and shared resource by comparing how much
water a person uses in the United States compared to someone
in a developing country. They then joined the World Water Day
March and walked a mile to experience firsthand how people in
the world must adapt without easy access to clean running water.
After these experiences, they created posters and performances to
raise awareness and educate parents, teachers, and peers about the
importance of water conservation.

Communicate ideas

Globally competent students can effectively communicate, verbally
and nonverbally, with diverse audiences. These students understand audiences that differ on the basis of culture, geography, faith,
ideology, wealth, and other factors and that these audiences may
perceive different meanings from the same information. Because
English is increasingly the world's language for commerce and
communication, globally competent students in the United States
and elsewhere are proficient in it, as well as in at least one other
world language. These students are also artistically and media
savvy; they know how to choose and effectively use appropriate
technology and media.

Students participating in the Global Kids Online Leadership
Program for teens wanted to educate their peers about global poverty. Working with a technology company, a group of high school
youth created a video game, *Ayiti: The Cost of Life*. Through the
game, online players learn about poverty by assuming virtual
responsibility for a fictional family in Haiti, making decisions
about when to send children to school versus work, and how to
spend scarce resources.

NEW DIRECTIONS FOR YOUTH DEVELOPMENT • DOI: 10.1002/yd

Take action

Globally competent students see themselves as actors, not bystanders. Alone or with others, they can creatively envision and weigh options for action based on evidence and insight and can assess the potential impact of each option, taking into account varied perspectives and potential consequences for others. Globally competent students demonstrate the courage both to act and to reflect on their actions.

Youth in a World Savvy after-school program at a Bronx, New York, high school wanted to explore the theme of immigration and identity. They started by researching the immigrant experience in their own community and identified an agency that helps support newcomer families. The young people went to the center and interviewed the staff of programs for immigrant children about what resources and support they needed. They used their arts skills to design T-shirts and other items to generate fundraising and then shared their knowledge of design through a workshop with students at the center.

Putting it in context

It is important to note that global competence requires applying these capacities across and within the academic disciplines. Globally competent students learn to think like historians or scientists or artists by using the tools of the disciplines to investigate the world, recognize perspectives, communicate ideas, and take action. Global competence also requires the ability to understand prevailing world conditions, issues, and trends through discipline-based and interdisciplinary learning.

Getting started with global learning in out-of-school time

Regardless of which age group you are working with, there is no shortage of approaches, topics, or themes when teaching about the world. After-school programs rely on hands-on experiences that keep young people engaged while expanding their horizons. One way to start integrating global content and curricula is to focus first on the specific approaches that are successful in the program already and then identify ways to apply them to global content— for example:

- *Project-based learning* starts with a question or problem that interests young people. As consumers, how might we be contributing to global poverty? Are there economic reasons that people pollute our planet? Can we stem the spread of global epidemics like malaria and tuberculosis? How can the world's largest producers of carbon emissions, the United States and China, work together on energy issues?
- *Object-based learning* uses objects to tell the stories of people, cultures, land, and environment. What is an object, such as a tool or a musical instrument, made of, and why is it made? Who first made it, and who uses it today? What does it reveal about life in its country of origin?
- *Field trips* in your community or another one, a museum, or a cultural institution build on what youth are learning. Think beyond four walls to the areas in your community that could be considered living museums—for example, a street full of markets, restaurants, clothing, and organizations from another part of the world.
- *Events, festivals, and celebrations* are a favorite way for after-school programs to bring in parents and the community and highlight traditions, food, and connections from around the world. They get participants excited about global learning and are also important entry points to more in-depth content knowledge.
- *Travel and exchanges* alter perspectives and expand vision. If young people do not have the opportunity to travel to other countries, you can help them travel virtually through technology and exchange experiences with peers in other places.
- *Guest speakers and artists in residence* can help bring local, cultural, and global connections to life, as well as provide insight into international careers. Colleges and universities can be useful

NEW DIRECTIONS FOR YOUTH DEVELOPMENT • DOI: 10.1002/yd

sources of international students and faculty, as well as local students who have recently returned from work and research abroad.

- *Internships and apprenticeships* attach young people to experts and professionals in a range of fields and build skills, career awareness, and connections for the future.

Expanding horizons through expanded learning

Leaders in school and afterschool can start by considering the strengths of their programs and how to approach them in a global context. Whether the after-school mission is academic achievement, enrichment, social and emotional skills, creativity, sports and health, or some combination of these, decide how the wider world relates to the entire educational experience of the participants in your program.

This process starts by assessing your current program to see where you can broaden your approach to connect to the twenty-first-century skills and global competence you want young people to achieve. Asia Society's Partnership for Global Learning offers a Global Learning in Afterschool Self-Assessment Tool that serves as a guide for programs that wish to bolster their program design, environment, activities, and policies to build global competence in youth.[5] For programs that are just getting started with global learning, the tool can be used as a framework for guiding preliminary discussions and to help identify areas of high-quality global learning in out-of-school time. More established programs can use the tool to measure progress to date and plot growth over time.

An important part of the self-assessment and action planning process is to explore how the global learning goals of an after-school or summer program might link to the school day. There are several possible approaches to consider:

- *A seamless connection between school and afterschool* can heighten global learning. School and after-school educators can share consistent goals, expectations, and practices. Curriculum maps and regular planning sessions can help educators align content to maximize impact for the benefit of youth. For example, if children are studying the Australian ecosystem in school, the after-school program might focus on aboriginal culture and the arts of Australia.

- *Complementary but separate roles between school and after-school programs* can support the acquisition of skills. Some after-school programs may have an international focus where the school itself does not. Nevertheless, after-school programs can still use global activities to reinforce skills covered during the school day. For example, if children are preparing for a language arts test, the program can concentrate on reading and writing using books with an international theme.

- *A focus on enrichment objectives distinct from the school day* can use the arts, languages, media and technology, sports, and play to create opportunities to develop twenty-first-century abilities, which can include everything from effective cross-cultural communication to collaborative teamwork, from creativity and innovation to critical thinking skills.

- *Summer programs* can offer immersive experiences and extended investigations of places, people, and global issues that connect to learning throughout the year. Summer is also an ideal time for in-depth exposure to world languages, community action projects, and travel.

One resource for further information and examples of globally focused afterschool and extended learning opportunities is *Expanding Horizons,* a guidebook published by Asia Society's Partnership for Global Learning that makes the case for integrating global learning into out-of-school time and provides a range of promising practices and resources.[6] The ideas and recommendations in the guide were drawn from a panel of expert advisors, interviews with more than one hundred leaders in the fields of after-school and international education, a review of materials and curricula, and site visits to after-school programs nationwide. A companion video, *Expanding Horizons,* narrated by CNN journalist Soledad O'Brien, introduces the importance of global learning and the unique role after-school programs can play.[7]

Young people need a range of educational experiences that help them expand their horizons beyond themselves to their communities, and from their communities to the rest of the world. A focus on global learning both during and after school can help advance academic achievement, social and emotional development, and civic engagement, providing young people with the critical skills they need to succeed.

Notes

1. Stewart, V. (2007). Becoming citizens of the world. *Educational Leadership, 64*(7), 8–14.

2. Conference Board. (2006). *Are they really ready to work? Employers' perspectives on the basic knowledge and applied skills of new entrants to the 21st century U.S. workforce.* Corporate Voices for Working Families, the Partnership for 21st Century Skills, and the Society for Human Resource Management. Retrieved from http://p21.org/documents/FINAL_REPORT_PDF09-29-06 .pdf; Committee for Economic Development. (2006). *Education for global leadership: The importance of international studies and foreign language education for U.S. economic and national security.* Washington, DC: Author. Retrieved from http://www.ced.org/images/library/reports/education/report _foreignlanguages.pdf.

3. Council of Chief State School Officers. EdSteps Project. Retrieved from http://www.edsteps.org/CCSSO/ManageContent.aspx?system_name= I5nka44NofDD3IY38QBonx+Crwfdw+uF&selected_system_name= DRkDdjiObdU=.

4. Mansilla, V. B., & Jackson, A. (2011). *Educating for global competence: Preparing our youth to engage the world.* Retrieved from http://asiasociety.org/files/ book-globalcompetence.pdf.

5. Asia Society. (2010). *Global learning in afterschool self-assessment tool.* Retrieved from http://sites.asiasociety.org/pgl2010/wp-content/uploads /2010/08/afterschool-assessment.pdf.

6. Asia Society. (2009a). *Expanding horizons: Building global literacy in afterschool programs.* Retrieved from http://asiasociety.org/node/9230.

7. Asia Society. (2009b). *Expanding horizons.* Video. Retrieved from http:// asiasociety.org/afterschool/video.

ALEXIS MENTEN *is associate director in Asia Society's Education division, where she leads after-school and youth leadership initiatives for the Partnership for Global Learning.*

An approach to theory-based youth programming

Mat D. Duerden, Ann Gillard

Abstract

A key but often overlooked aspect of intentional, out-of-school-time programming is the integration of a guiding theoretical framework. The incorporation of theory in programming can provide practitioners valuable insights into essential processes and principles of successful programs. While numerous theories exist that relate to youth development practice, they often remain inaccessible to practitioners. Therefore, the goal of this article is to synthesize two theoretical perspectives, the social development model and self-determination theory, into a practitioner-friendly programming framework. The resulting social development programming model outlines specific components, processes, and outcomes of effective and intentional youth development programs.

TO BE SUCCESSFUL, out-of-school-time programs must intentionally target specific outcomes. One effective approach for developing intentional programs is to integrate a theoretical framework into the programming process. Numerous theories exist that could potentially inform youth development practice, but they often remain shrouded from practitioners behind an aura of academic inaccessibility. This is unfortunate because many theories naturally lend themselves to real-world applications. In an effort to address the research to practice gap, this article introduces an out-of-school-time programming model based on proven theoretical frameworks to facilitate the development of theory-based youth programs.

NEW DIRECTIONS FOR YOUTH DEVELOPMENT, SUPPLEMENT 2011 © WILEY PERIODICALS, INC.
Published online in Wiley Online Library (wileyonlinelibrary.com) • DOI: 10.1002/yd.418

The benefit of a theory-based programming model is that it does not dictate exact practices but rather organizes principles and processes into a coherent structure that produces, when implemented correctly, intended outcomes. This approach is more effective than suggesting a laundry list of promising practices without an underlying rationale for how they relate to each other or what type of outcomes they might produce. For example, some practices might prove effective only in certain contexts, whereas principles can guide the development of context-specific promising practices. In other words, a programming model provides practitioners with a governing framework that unifies purposes and provides direction as they develop practices tailored to their own programs.

To be successful, a youth program must be both intentional enough to produce desired outcomes and simple enough to be correctly implemented by staff and volunteers. The proposed social development programming model (SDPM) meets these requirements and can help practitioners develop a more theory-based approach to youth programming. The SDPM is designed to provide a clear representation of the principles and practices essential for developing quality programs. It also links all programming efforts into a unified, intentional focus on key, targeted outcomes.

The SDPM represents a combination of two theoretical perspectives: the social development model and self-determination theory.[1] The common thread of these perspectives is their focus on clarifying key processes and components of positive developmental contexts and experiences.

_____

Social development model

The social developmental model (SDM; see Figure 1) provides a theoretical approach to understanding the impact of relationships and socialization on behavior.[2] The model suggests that individuals develop bonds to groups and organizations when they experience opportunities for involvement, possess the necessary skills for

NEW DIRECTIONS FOR YOUTH DEVELOPMENT • DOI: 10.1002/yd

Figure 1. Social development model

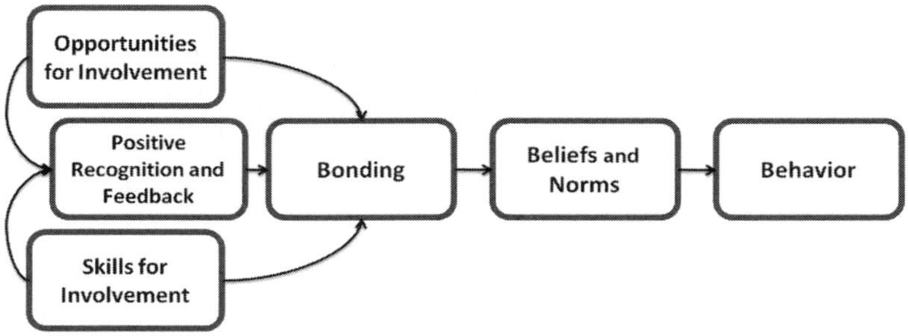

Source: Adapted from Hawkins and Weis (1985).

involvement, and receive positive feedback regarding said involvement.[3] Bonding usually leads individuals to adopting the norms and expectations of the group.[4] The SDM has been validated and proven to have predictive qualities in a variety of settings.[5]

The SDM serves as the core of the SDPM. It provides a clear and validated pathway between the experiences youth have within program contexts and targeted beliefs and behaviors. The model highlights the importance of relationships and socialization as the processes whereby positive change occurs. In programming terms, the emphasis is on relationships, with the activities serving as vehicles for positive socialization. It is important to note that research and field experience suggest that not all opportunities for involvement are created equally. For example, in a mixed-methods evaluation of an international immersion program for adolescents, researchers, based on the study's findings, suggested that the best opportunities for involvement create space for socially equal relationships between youth and adults to develop.[6]

Self-determination theory

Self-determination theory (SDT) provides additional insights regarding key motivational processes and psychological needs associated with positive development contexts. SDT examines the psychological processes that occur within social contexts and how these processes influence one's reasons or motivation to act or behave. SDT suggests that when people are self-determined, they feel free to do what is interesting, significant, and enlivening for them. SDT outlines six types of motivation, ranging from motivations to do something because of forces external to the self and lacking internal values, to intrinsic motivation that occurs when the activity is inherently satisfying, enjoyable, and in line with one's value system. When people experience self-determination, they are intrinsically motivated rather than externally motivated (doing something for reward or to avoid punishment) or amotivated (not wanting to do something for any reason). The development of intrinsically motivated behavior is integral to human development.[7] Intrinsically motivated activities prepare youth for adulthood through tasks that develop self-direction, self-expression, and motivated involvement.[8]

SDT also suggests that contexts that promote the basic needs of autonomy, competence, and relatedness are those where internalized motivations will emerge and that these needs are fundamental and innate for all people. *Autonomy* refers to the need to feel volition or self-control in one's actions. Those who have choice can use available information to regulate themselves in the achievement of goals. *Relatedness* refers to people's needs to connect with others and form a sense of belonging to something bigger than themselves. *Competence* refers to people's needs to feel self-efficacious, to believe that they are the cause of their actions, and to receive informational and useful feedback that enhances their intrinsic motivation. Whereas competence is required for any type of motivation and relatedness comes from internalizing the norms and values of the social group, autonomy is also needed for the motivation to be intrinsic.[9] When the basic needs for autonomy, relatedness, and competence are met, self-determination is optimized. Favorable social contexts that support these needs are those that contain informative (not controlling) feedback and support from trusted others. This feedback can be competence based ("She knows what she's talking about") or relationship based ("I like him, so I will listen to what he says").

Social supports can enhance well-being because they fulfill basic needs.[10] Feelings of relatedness are vital for internalization and integration of the values associated with an activity because the desire to connect with significant others is an essential component of people's willingness to endorse such values.[11] A sense of belonging is an essential factor for youth to internalize positive beliefs about themselves and others. Out-of-school-time programs can provide social supports and their associated nutriments to meet youths' basic needs.

Incorporating SDT into the SDPM provides guidance regarding the inherent qualities of opportunities most likely to lead to bonding. Youth programs need to be intentionally designed to promote participants' autonomy, relatedness, and competence.

Social development programming model

The SDPM (see Figure 2) uses the general components and relationships of the SDM as its foundation. The framework also incorporates SDT because it provides insights into the qualitative nature of high quality program experiences. The SDPM consists of two main sections: within-program components and processes and resulting outcomes. The first section proposes that programs need to be structured in order to provide opportunities for youth involvement, positive relationships and recognition, and the development and application of skills. When this happens participants' basic psychological needs, such as autonomy, relatedness, and competence, are met, and therefore they will be more likely to develop a bond to the youth program, leaders, and peers.[12] The second section outlines what happens as a result of this bonding. Research suggests that bonding leads to the adoption of the group's norms and that norms in turn influence future behavior.[13] In the case of out-of-school-time programs, this would mean youth would adopt the positive norms or standards of the organization (for a youth sports program, for example, this could be positive sportsmanship) and be more likely to act according to these

Figure 2. Social development programming model

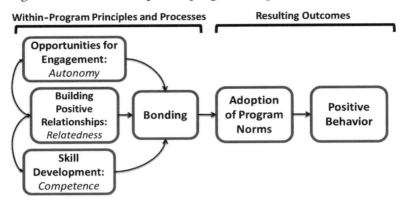

beliefs. The following sections provide a more detailed look at each of the components of the SDPM.

Building positive relationships

Relationships between youth and adult leaders are one of the most, if not the most, important components of youth programs.[14] Accordingly, the primary focus of most youth activities should be on building positive relationships. In the youth development literature, the distinction is made between relationship- and activity-based programming.[15] Leaders often get so wrapped up in the mechanics of running a program that they do not have sufficient time or energy left over for relationship building. Research, however, has shown that atmosphere, not activities, is the best predictor of program success and that leaders who first build positive relationships have an increased ability to promote positive behavior and development.[16]

Not only does the focus need to be on building relationships but on certain types of relationships. Adults often hold preconceived attitudes about youth that can lead to the development of less effective relationships.[17] Counterproductive relationships develop when adults judge youth based on personal biases rather than actual interactions (for example, saying, "He's just a skater kid"). Prescriptive relationships occur when adults have a predetermined agenda for fixing a youth before even trying to get to know him or her. Adult leaders need to be encouraged to first get to know their youth and build trusting relationships before trying to "fix problems." It is difficult to help anyone without first sincerely trying to understand his or her perspective.

Research suggests that leaders who help meet their youths' needs for autonomy, relatedness, and competence are more likely to develop positive relationships with youth.[18] Accordingly, the successful application of the SDPM will help facilitate positive relationships. In addition, it is important for youth and adults to have more horizontal rather than vertical interactions. Youth and adults often interact in a top-down fashion, with adults having full control or power over the situation. Meaningful relationships are more likely to result when youth and adults have opportunities for shared experiences that are more socially equal.[19] For example, relationships that develop when youth and adults jointly participate as equals in a meaningful activity are much different from activities consisting of only vertical interactions. Adults should still maintain control and structure over activities, but they need to seek more opportunities to level the playing field.

Finally, it is imperative that youth be allowed to build sustained relationships with their adult leaders. Relationships that last longer than a year are most effective and some research even suggests that short-term relationships can be detrimental, leading to feelings of abandonment.[20]

An example: Although it is important to allow youth to play a lead role in the development and implementation of the programs, this does not mean a leader's role is to sit on the sideline. Leaders should work to recognize opportunities for meaningful interactions with youth. During activities, leaders should not avoid becoming a passive observer or spend their time interacting with other adults in the program. Actively participating with the youth provides excellent opportunities for building positive relationships.

NEW DIRECTIONS FOR YOUTH DEVELOPMENT • DOI: 10.1002/yd

Opportunities for engagement

Not just any activities promote bonding and positive relationships. Youth become engaged and show more initiative when they feel their opinions are valued and that they have some choice in what is going on the program.[21] This is referred to as *youth voice*. Youth need opportunities to have their opinions heard in ways that matter and affect change. Superficial attempts to promote youth voice should be avoided. Youth will quickly recognize if their opinions are asked for but not acted upon.[22] Although it requires more work to promote youth voice, it is an essential component of effective youth programs.

An example: Creating opportunities for engagement can be as simple as asking youth about their interests, talents, and hobbies. This knowledge allows leaders to work with youth to incorporate their individual interests into the program.

Skill development

Intentional programming decisions should be made regarding the key skills and assets youth need to navigate adolescence successfully. A fairly established body of literature exists regarding the developmental assets youth need in order to become successful adults. For example, the Search Institute has identified and validated the efficacy of forty developmental assets youth need to thrive.[23] This list is divided into subcategories organized into internal (for example, commitment to learning, positive values, social competencies, and positive identity) and external (for example, support, empowerment, boundaries and expectations, and constructive use of time) asset domains.[24]

To identify key assets associated with their programs, practitioners can look for overlap between the forty developmental assets and their organization's targeted skills. For example, a service-learning program would naturally develop the asset of giving service to others; with some additional intentionality, it could also add components to facilitate the development of related assets like planning, decision making, and cultural competence. As youth increase their skill abilities within the program, there is a good chance that this growth will spill over into other contexts.

Self-efficacy theory suggests that one of the best ways to have an influence on future behavior is to increase individuals' confidence in their abilities to complete tasks associated with a targeted behavior. The theory additionally notes that growth in one context can often generalize to others.[25] Accordingly, if a participant develops decision-making skills in an out-of-school-time program, he or she may also experience an increased ability to apply that skill in school activities. Skill development within programs is a key aspect of the SDPM because it requires programmers to intentionally structure experiences to help youth progress in their development.

An example: Sports and physical activities are often an integral and rewarding aspect of many youth programs. Rather than simply playing basketball or soccer, however, consider incorporating skill-building activities as well. This can help youth who may not feel as physically skilled as others to develop greater competence and allow more skilled youth opportunities to teach and serve. A skill-building exercise before playing the game can make the overall experience more beneficial for youth of all skill levels.

Bonding

When youth have the opportunity to participate in activities that meet their needs for autonomy, relatedness, and competence; when they possess and apply the needed skills for involvement; and when they receive positive feedback for doing so, they bond to the program. Bonding is powerful because it also leads to the adoption of organizational beliefs and norms. The efficacy of bonding has been shown in school contexts where increased bonding is associated with improved academic performance and school behavior.[26]

An example: After-school programs can rally neighborhood, cultural, or other types of groups in identifying and celebrating the qualities that make the group and the program unique. Such efforts could include exhibits, parades, festivals, open houses, and more. Through this process, bonding occurs through the establishment of a collective empowered identity. Additionally, youth who are bonded with the program are less likely to quit or cause disruptions, and more likely to experience active engagement with the program activities and people.

Adoption of program norms

As youth bond to the program, they need to have a clear idea of the beliefs and norms of the sponsoring organization. This requires that those in the organization first have a clear idea of what norms they espouse and promote. This awareness, coupled with bonding, is more likely to lead to the adoption of these norms. Youth leaders need to live and teach these norms in their interactions with the youth they work with so these young people will develop a desire to emulate their behavior. Clear statements of organizational beliefs should be incorporated in all aspects of program to provide consistent reinforcement.

Positive behavior

The positive behavior resulting from bonding to the organization and adoption of its beliefs and norms represent the final component of the social development programming model. Specific outcome behaviors will differ across programs depending on organizational beliefs and norms. The identification of program outcomes should be the first step of SDPM guided program development. Norms and belief should clearly connect to outcomes and all activities should be geared toward realizing outcomes. The SDPM provides an intentional pathway to reach outcomes, but these outcomes must be clearly communicated to youth leaders so they can have a clear end goal in all that they do. It is important to note that the SDPM does not dictate outcomes but rather organizes principles into a framework to produce targeted outcomes.

Training individuals to use the youth programming model

Research suggests that well-trained staff are key to successful youth programs.[27] One of the strongest predictors of youth worker effectiveness is not the person's level of previous experience or shared characteristics he or she has with the youth, but rather his or her confidence in working with youth. Although this confidence may come naturally for some, it can be developed in all individuals through training. Thus, it should not be surprising that a proven key aspect of effective mentoring programs is quality ongoing training for adult mentors.[28] Unfortunately, many adults who work in youth programs receive little or no training for this work.

Some research suggests that when adults lack training or a clear idea of what their role as a youth leader entails, they revert to the standard adult role of the disciplinarian.[29] In this role, their main interactions with the youth occur to "keep kids in line" rather than build positive relationships. It can be hard for a new youth leader to engage and work with youth. Young people can seem intimidating, and even scary, and it is not uncommon for individuals to feel unclear about how they should interact with youth. This can also be a problem if the focus is put on activities rather than relationships because adults may hold off from interacting with the youth for fear of disrupting the activity. Fortunately, many of these issues can be remedied through proper training. Research suggests that even short-term training can have a significant positive impact on adults' abilities to work with youth.[30]

Staff training is most effective when it is grounded in a guiding framework such as the SDPM. The SDPM provides the principles on which the training curriculum can be built. Youth leaders who understand the framework will gain insight into the types of activities they should develop, how best to develop relationships with their youth, and how to engage youth more fully in their programming. They will then have the ability to create a youth program that encompasses the components and processes of the SDPM, thereby more effectively facilitating the positive development of their youth and the promotion of a program's targeted outcomes.

From a programming perspective, the SDPM can be thought of as a structured logic model.[31] Accordingly, programmers should start at the end of the model by identifying desired behavioral outcomes and then work toward the beginning. For example, a program with an environmental education focus could target recycling as a desired end behavior. They would then need to promote program beliefs and norms conducive to promoting recycling. Once these pieces are in place, decisions can be made about structuring the program itself to provide opportunities for youth involvement, positive relationships and recognition, and the development and application of skills in line with targeted outcomes.

Conclusion

This article has presented a preliminary proposal for a framework to guide youth programming. It is based on sound theory and research and is designed to produce targeted outcomes. It promotes the communication of unified goals and application of principles while leaving specific program practices up to individual leaders, who best understand the contexts in which their programs operate. It also provides a framework for youth practitioner trainings. Out-of-school-time programs are more than fun and games, but in order to offer truly transformative experiences, they must be intentional. Building programs on sound theoretical foundations facilitates intentional programming, but the incorporation of theory can be difficult because it requires a certain level of familiarity with applicable frameworks in order to use them effectively. The SDPM can help bridge this gap and provide practitioners a tool for creating programs to promote positive youth development.

Notes

1. For the social development model: Catalano, R. F., & Hawkins, J. D. (1996). The social development model: A theory of antisocial behavior. In J. D. Hawkins (Ed.), *Delinquency and crime: Current theories* (pp. 149–197). Cambridge: Cambridge University Press; Hawkins, J. D., & Weis, J. G. (1985). The social development model: An integrated approach to delinquency prevention. *Journal of Primary Prevention*, *6*(2), 73–97. For self-determination theory: Ryan, R. M., & Deci, E. L. (2000). Self-determination theory and the facilitation of intrinsic motivation, social development, and well-being. *American Psychologist*, *55*(1), 68–78.

2. Catalano & Hawkins. (1996); Hawkins & Weis. (1985).

3. Hawkins, J. D., Catalano, R. F., & Arthur, M. W. (2002). Promoting science-based prevention in communities. *Addictive Behaviors*, *27*(6), 951–976.

4. Catalano & Hawkins. (1996).

5. Catalano, R. F., Haggerty, K. P., Oesterle, S., Fleming, C. B., & Hawkins, J. D. (2004). The importance of bonding to school for healthy development: Findings from the Social Development Research Group. *Journal of School Health*, *74*(7), 252–261; Catalano, R. F., Oxford, M. L., Harachi, T. W., Abbott, R. D., & Haggerty, K. P. (1999). A test of the social development model to predict problem behaviour during the elementary school period. *Criminal Behaviour and Mental Health*, *9*, 39–56; Duerden, M. D., & Witt, P. A. (2010). The impact of socialization on youth program outcomes: A social development model perspective. *Leisure Sciences*, *32*(4), 299–317.

6. Duerden & Witt. (2010).

7. Ryan & Deci. (2000).

8. Larson, R. W., & Kleiber, D. (1993). Daily experience of adolescents. In P. Tolan & B. Cohler (Eds.), *Handbook of clinical research and practice with adolescents* (pp. 125–145). Hoboken, NJ: Wiley.

9. Ryan & Deci. (2000).

10. Ryan, R. M., & Solky, J. A. (1996). What is supportive about social support? On the psychological needs for autonomy and relatedness. In G. R. Pierce, B. R. Sarason, & I. G. Sarason (Eds.), *Handbook of social support and the family* (pp. 249–267). New York, NY: Plenum Press.

11. Ryan & Deci. (2000).

12. Ryan & Deci. (2000).

13. Lonczak, H. S., Huang, B., Catalano, R. F., Hawkins, J. D., Hill, K. G., Abbott, R. D., . . . Kosterman, R. (2001). The social predictors of adolescent alcohol misuse: A test of the social development model. *Journal of Studies on Alcohol*, *62*(2), 179–189.

14. Yohalem, N., Granger, R. C., & Pittman, K. J. (2009). The quest for quality: Recent developments and future directions for the out-of-school-time field. In N. Yohalem, R. C. Granger, & K. J. Pittman (Eds.), *Defining and Measuring Quality in Youth Programs and Classrooms. New Directions for Youth Development*, *121*, 129–140. doi:10.1002/yd.300.

15. Bocarro, J. N., & Witt, P. A. (2005). The power of people: Relationship-based programming. In P. A. Witt & L. L. Caldwell (Eds.), *Recreation and adolescent development* (pp. 266–280). State College, PA: Venture.

16. Roth, J. L., & Brooks-Gunn, J. (2003). Youth development programs: Risk, prevention and policy. *Journal of Adolescent Health, 32*(3), 170–182. doi:10.1207/S1532480XADS0702_6

17. Bocarro & Witt. (2005).

18. Duerden, M. D., & Gillard, A. (2008–2009, Winter). Promoting supportive relationships in youth programs: A self-determination theory perspective. *Journal of Youth Development, 3*(3). Retrieved from http://www.nae4ha.org/directory/jyd/jyd_article.aspx?id=e341422c-1fc5-46cf-9da6-603693e6a110.

19. Duerden & Witt. (2010).

20. Grossman, J. B., & Rhodes, J. E. (2002). The test of time: Predictors and effects of duration in youth mentoring relationships. *American Journal of Community Psychology, 30*(2), 199–219. doi: 10.1023/A:1014680827552

21. Herrera, C., Sipe, C. L., McClanahan, W. S., & Arbreton, A. J. A. (2000). *Relationship development in community-based and school-based programs.* Philadelphia, PA: Public/Private Ventures.

22. Ellis, J. M., & Caldwell, L. L. (2005). Increasing youth voice. In P. A. Witt & L. L. Caldwell (Eds.), *Recreation and youth development* (pp. 281–299). State College, PA: Venture Publishing.

23. Benson, P. L. (2006). *All kids are our kids: What communities must do to raise caring and responsible children and adolescents* (2nd ed.). San Francisco, CA: Jossey-Bass.

24. For more information on the Search Institute's forty assets, see www.searchinstitute.org.

25. Bandura, A. (1997). *Self-efficacy: The exercise of control.* New York, NY: Freeman.

26. Catalano et al. (2004).

27. DuBois, D. L., Holloway, B. E., Valentine, J. C., & Cooper, H. (2002). Effectiveness of mentoring programs for youth: A meta-analytic review. *American Journal of Community Psychology, 30*(2), 157–197. doi:10.1023/A:1014628810714; Tierney, J. P., Grossman, J. B., & Resch, N. L. (1995). *Making a difference: An impact study of Big Brothers/Big Sisters.* Philadelphia, PA: Public/Private Ventures.

28. DuBois et al. (2002).

29. Duerden & Witt. (2010).

30. Smoll, F. L., Smith, R. E., Barnett, N. P., & Everett, J. J. (1993). Enhancement of children's self-esteem through social support training for youth sport coaches. *Journal of Applied Psychology, 78*(4), 602–610. doi:10.1037/0021–9010.78.4.602

31. Baldwin, C. K., Caldwell, L. L., & Witt, P. A. (2005). Deliberate programming with logic models: From theory to outcomes. In P. A. Witt & L. L. Caldwell (Eds.), *Recreation and youth development* (pp. 219–237). State College, PA: Venture Publishing.

MAT D. DUERDEN *is an assistant professor and extension specialist in the Department of Recreation, Park and Tourism Sciences at Texas A&M University. He is also the coordinator of the Sequor Youth Development Initiative at Texas A&M.*

ANN GILLARD *is an assistant professor of youth development in the Department of Social Sciences at Springfield College in Massachusetts.*

The importance of mentoring relationships among youth workers

Julianne Gassman, Michael C. Gleason

Abstract

Organizational leaders often work to retain their employees and teach them the knowledge needed in becoming future organizational leaders. The purpose of the study examined in this article was to determine how mentoring within Camp Adventure Child and Youth Services contributes to the development of students selected to deliver programs to children and youth worldwide. Strong evidence of mentoring and development were found in both the training and delivery of services. The results of this study are meaningful not only for the particular program studied but for all youth-serving organizations. Supervisors and administrators of youth-serving organizations should be intentional about developing and promoting healthy mentoring relationships to create positive environments for staff and the youth being served.

ORGANIZATIONS MUST OPERATE in increasingly complex environments with constant pressure to function with fewer resources. Organizational leaders are often expected to meet external demands as well as the many needs of the employees working within the organization. Organizations that are able to retain individuals as they learn more about the organization and develop these individuals as leaders can affect the capacity and quality of services provided. It is therefore in the best interest of organizational leaders to understand how to support employees and most effective leadership development practices with employees.[1] Youth-serving organizations specifically stand to benefit from

NEW DIRECTIONS FOR YOUTH DEVELOPMENT, SUPPLEMENT 2011 © WILEY PERIODICALS, INC.
Published online in Wiley Online Library (wileyonlinelibrary.com) • DOI: 10.1002/yd.419

learning and understanding how developing their youth workers can be beneficial to the workers themselves and the organization.

The literature related to the importance of mentoring youth is expansive; however, mentoring relationships that develop between and among youth workers themselves have not been as thoroughly explored. Researchers of one study on leadership distributed surveys to over three hundred for-profit and nonprofit leaders to better understand what leaders of organizations valued most in other leaders. The study found that the top three competencies most important to leaders are honesty and integrity, working collaboratively, and developing others.[2] Since mentoring is an important method used in developing others and because the development of youth workers is an important component of youth programs, the focus of this study is on mentoring relationships among youth workers and the impact of these relationships on the personal development of youth workers, as well as on the advancement of youth programs as a whole.

Supervision and mentoring

Mentoring behaviors often take place within the context of the supervisory relationships of organizations. There are many supervision models, yet several common themes emerge: developing others, helping the organization achieve goals, and improving instruction and delivery.[3] Similar functions can be found within the context of mentoring relationships. In addition, many of the attributes of effective supervision, such as trust building, sharing of values, and sensitivity are found within mentoring.[4] Therefore, overlap in behaviors and goals of mentoring and supervision is found.

Supervision, however, can be found without mentoring taking place. This can be partially attributed to the fact that supervisors are often promoted because of their technical skills, knowledge, and experience in a particular field rather than their ability to manage and develop others. Often supervisors are not trained in the area of developing skills in others but are promoted because of their own abilities[5] In addition, supervisors have the added responsibilities of taking factors such as the organization's mission and the clients served into decision making and practice, whereas mentors can focus primarily on the development of their protégés and may not have the organization or its clients at the forefront of the relationship.[6] This study explores mentoring relationships within the confines of a supervisory structure and beyond the typical hierarchical relationship.

Mentoring: A review of the literature

Mentoring is a vital feature of organizations and one method by which organizational members can work to develop the leadership abilities of coworkers. Organizational mentoring has three major benefits for individuals. Mentoring assists both individuals and organizations in doing better work by enhancing motivation and learning, and by demonstrating and teaching organizational norms, values, and opportunities.[7] And it has bidirectional benefits: it benefits not only those being mentored but also those serving as mentors. The importance of sharing these benefits with employees as leaders work to develop mentoring programs within organizations is an important point of reference in the literature.[8] When successful mentoring practices take place, both those being mentored and those mentoring find the experience worthwhile.

Mentoring can take on varied meanings within different organizations and in differing social contexts. If mentoring is to be successful, it must be carefully tailored to fit within the culture of the organization. In addition, certain components must exist for a true mentoring relationship to form. The two vital components of any mentoring relationship are reciprocity and the willingness of each party to grow and change.[9] Mentoring is dependent on one person's ability to seek a mentor and another person's willingness to serve as a mentor.[10] It is a "dynamic, reciprocal relationship in a work environment between an advanced career incumbent [mentor] and a beginner [protégé] aimed at promoting the career development of both."[11] Supervisors and their subordinates often reciprocate and demonstrate a willingness to grow and change in their relationship together; however, as this study finds, this agreement can also be found among peers and in other nonsupervisor relationships.

Mentoring can be formal or informal. In formal mentoring programs, organizational members are officially paired and recognized as mentoring pairs by others. Informal mentoring relationships exist when one member of the organization informally chooses another member as a mentor or protégé without official recognition by the organization.

Overwhelmingly, the literature related to mentoring describes the more traditional perspective of those with more experience mentoring those with less experience.[12] In traditional mentoring relationships, the mentor is in a higher position of status or power within the organizational structure than the protégé, such as that found between a supervisor and supervisee. However, many mentoring relationships today, often known as peer mentoring relationships, comprise two people within the same tier of the organization. One researcher describes peer mentoring as an intentional relationship between two employees. Although the employees may be at the same level in the organization, the one with more experience teaches the newer employee knowledge and skills to enhance his or her performance.[13]

No matter what form mentoring relationships take, the benefits are influential to those in the relationship, as well as to the organization as whole. Mentoring has a large number of benefits for individuals. A summary of these benefits to those serving as mentors include success on the job, recognition for their work, a compensation increase, and career satisfaction. Individuals also have feelings of rejuvenation from mentoring, as well as see an increase in promotions and gain more power and access to important information.[14]

There is also a psychosocial benefit for individuals. The psychosocial functions of a mentoring relationship enhance the protégés' sense of competence, confidence, effectiveness, and esteem. In addition the friendships formed and informal interactions promote a willingness to discuss a variety of topics that may otherwise go unaddressed. Mentoring helps protégés in the development of strategies necessary in the workplace and also gives an opportunity for informal feedback they may not otherwise receive. The need people have for cooperation and sharing personal values is more likely to be met when mentoring relationships exist.[15]

There are organizational benefits that relate to mentoring as well. Mentoring can increase the effective socialization of employees and supports employees in being more committed to their jobs and careers. In addition, it helps decrease staff turnover.[16] Mentoring not only relates to career advancement and skill development but also provides strong, continuous emotional support that is beneficial for the organization.[17] Mentoring can increase the capacity of organizations and the knowledge of its workers in a variety of ways. It facilitates understanding the need for having standards of quality, promotes quality in performance, improves application of knowledge, encourages confidence in problem solving, and strengthens individuals to be motivated to do their best.[18] An increase in knowledge sharing promotes an increase in knowledge creation and development as well as aids in the process of building intellectual capital.[19]

Mentoring can serve as a tool to educate employees on the organization's culture and socialize them on how to be successful within that culture. In addition, formal mentoring relationships can be of use when transferring management styles and approaches.[20] Supervisees who identify their supervisors as mentors often adopt the methods of management and leadership that their overseer demonstrates. Another vitally important function of mentoring is as a stress reliever. The relationship between the mentor and protégé allows conversation and the ability to relieve stress related to the job.[21] This stress relief is a benefit not only for the individual but for the organization as a whole because the cost of employee stress can be financial for the organization and detrimental to an individual's health.

Understanding the benefits of mentoring alone is insufficient in creating atmospheres conducive to the practice. A number of organizational characteristics can contribute to the potential for the success of the relationship. It is important for organizations to have a cooperative context.[22] Productive mentoring can exist only when all those involved place a high priority on constructive relationships. Members of the organization must be open to working with each other in a friendly manner where feelings and thoughts are shared for the benefit of each other and the organization. Supervisors and administrators must establish this supportive environment. This type of environment can be conducive to the creation of healthy mentoring relationships, formal or informal, because of the amount of support, trust, and sharing of knowledge that exists within the organization.

Although dismissal of the role of the institution or organization in the success of any mentoring program should not occur, it is important to remember that ultimately the attitudes that the mentor and protégé bring to the relationship are most important. A review of the work of a well-known mentoring researcher found mutual liking of each other to be key to the development of a productive, healthy mentoring relationship.[23] The overarching concept that can be drawn from the research is that leaders within any organization can work to develop mechanisms conducive to mentoring.

For this study, we assume that mentoring relationships exist whenever two or more individuals operating within the organization interact in ways that increase either individual's chance of success within the organization. This study focuses on the mentoring relationships in a youth-serving organization and examines the mentoring that exists during the time staff are being trained and during program delivery.

Context of the study

Camp Adventure Child and Youth Services (CACYS) is a youth-serving organization headquartered at the University of Northern

Iowa. It contracts with U.S. military bases and installations, embassies, international schools, and parks and recreation departments to provide child and youth programs in child development centers, school-age-care programs, and teen and aquatics programs. CACYS recruits college and university students, screens them for participation, and trains those it hires through its staff development program. The main objective of this organization is to provide educational experiences for college and university students while delivering quality child and youth programs worldwide. Approximately eight hundred college students participate every year.

Training is facilitated at twelve staff development locations: Washington State University, University of Oregon, California State University at Davis, California State University at Chico, University of San Diego, Fort Valley State University, Florida A&M University, Paine College, University of Toledo, Iowa State University, University of Iowa, and the University of Northern Iowa. Every student must complete the staff development program at one of these locations. Each staff development program is managed by a lead trainer with the support of an assistant trainer. Each trainee is part of a group facilitated by a group leader. Once students successfully complete the staff development program, they are assigned to a program to deliver services to children and youth. Most are assigned to a program on a U.S. military installation to supplement existing staff in school-age care, providing summer camp programs for military dependent children.

The purpose of this study was to determine how mentoring within CACYS contributes to the development of the college and university students selected to deliver programs to children and youth. Participants were chosen because of their participation in CACYS day camps during summer 2008. CACYS operates in seven major regions: the continental United States, Hawaii, northern Europe, southern Europe, Korea, mainland Japan, and Okinawa, Japan. The researchers surveyed individuals from each of the hierarchical levels within the organization—counselor, program director, project coordinator, and project director—and from

NEW DIRECTIONS FOR YOUTH DEVELOPMENT • DOI: 10.1002/yd

six of the seven regions listed. Counselors work directly with the children, program directors lead one program and are not typically working directly with the children, project coordinators manage approximately five or six programs within their area, and project directors manage an entire region such as Korea or Japan. Students participating in programs in the United States were not included because one of the researchers was a supervisor in this region.

CACYS participants in summer 2008 were surveyed about their experiences with both the staff development program and their summer experience when they were considered "on the job." To determine how involved participants were with both those they supervised and their own supervisors, questions related to interactions with these individuals were incorporated into the survey. Questions related to the content and context of these interactions were also created to determine if relationships during the staff development program and during the summer were indeed of a mentoring nature.

Surveys were used to determine how mentoring affected the development and growth of the participants. The survey incorporated the perspectives of individuals from a variety of staff development programs, summer locations, and positions held in the organization. The researchers incorporated questions that related to the frequency and type of interaction between trainers and trainees during staff development, as well as supervisors and supervisees during the summer to determine if mentoring relationships existed between these individuals. Questions were also constructed to determine if the relationship that an individual had with another organizational member was reciprocal in nature.

It was important to determine which individuals surveyed felt their performance had improved throughout the summer, associating some type of learning with their summer experience. Therefore, questions related to learning were incorporated. To understand which individuals throughout program participation acted as mentors, the final question in the survey explicitly asked this question.

NEW DIRECTIONS FOR YOUTH DEVELOPMENT • DOI: 10.1002/yd

The survey was analyzed through comparison of survey responses to characteristics typical of mentoring relationships. The survey had been constructed based on a literary foundation of mentoring and thus gauged the extent to which individuals were mentored or mentored others. The researchers also used survey responses in the calculation of descriptive statistics of the population surveyed.

Results and interpretation

Of the 396 individuals who were invited to participate due to their participation in a school-age care program during summer 2008, 174 completed the survey, for a response rate of 43.9 percent. Of the 174 individuals who began the survey, 150, or 86 percent, completed the survey. Since each question could be answered or left unanswered, participation rates by question varied. That is, all percentages are based on the number who answered the particular question.

Respondents were mostly female. Of those who responded, 14.5 percent (24) were male and 85.5 percent (142) were female. Like many other organizations within child and youth care settings, females heavily represent CACYS. Over half of the respondents (56 percent, or 93 individuals) were first-time participants in CACYS. The remaining 44 percent were students with experience ranging from second-time participation to twelfth-time participation. Finally, it is important to note that CACYS does not have a formal mentoring program, and all answers indicate mentoring relationships that developed informally.

Responses indicate that individuals at all levels of the organization, during the staff development program and during the summer, were viewed as mentors. Figures 1 and 2 display the percentage of survey respondents who felt mentored by particular individuals throughout the staff development program and during the summer. Ninety-two percent (145) of respondents felt mentored by someone during the staff development program.

Sixty-eight percent (106) of individuals felt their lead trainer had served as a mentor during training (Figure 1), while almost half of the respondents felt their project coordinator or program director mentored them during the summer (Figure 2).

Figure 1. Percentage of survey respondents who felt these individuals acted as mentors during the staff development program

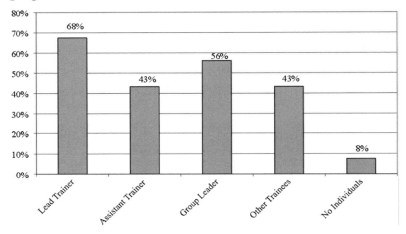

Figure 2. Percentage of respondents who felt these individuals acted as mentors during the summer

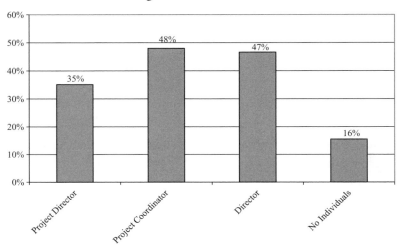

Lead trainers should understand the importance of their role not only as trainers but also as mentors who influence the behaviors and actions of their trainees. Since training is typically one of the first experiences for a new participant or employee, the lead trainer has the responsibility for communicating the values and traditions of the organization. The lead trainer may be one of the first to explore the culture of the organization with the new employee. In addition, almost half of the respondents saw other trainees as mentors, indicating that peer mentoring is prevalent in the organization. Shared learning was common among new participants, possibly drawing them toward each other for support. During program implementation, mentoring relationships continue, as demonstrated in Figure 2. Program directors and project coordinators are seen as mentors by almost half of the respondents, indicating that direct supervisors of new participants or employees have great influence.

Individuals were also asked about their mentoring of others during the summer when implementing the program. Of those who felt they served as a mentor to someone during the summer, 17.9 percent (seven respondents) felt they had mentored project coordinators, 41 percent (sixteen respondents) felt they had mentored program directors, 94.9 percent (thirty-seven respondents) felt that they had mentored counselors, and 2.6 percent (one respondent) felt they had mentored no one (see Figure 3). It should be recognized that almost everyone felt he or she had acted as a mentor to someone, most indicating they had mentored a counselor, typically a new participant. This likely means that everyone feels as though he or she has something to contribute to the development of others, especially new participants. Results also indicate that individuals feel they mentor others in management roles in the organization.

Responses indicate that communication between supervisors and those they supervised was frequent. In addition, the majority of those who supervised others felt that they had taught those they supervised something and that those who were supervised felt they learned something from their supervisor. Respondents were asked

Figure 3. Percentage of respondents who felt they acted as mentors for these individuals

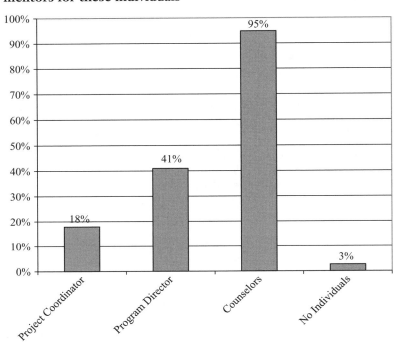

to rate whether they agreed with five statements related to learning and improvement during the summer. Figure 4 indicates the percentage of respondents who agreed with the respective statement based on their supervisor's influence. Figure 5 demonstrates the percentage of those who agreed with the respective statement based on their learning from those they supervised.

Seventy-nine percent (116) of respondents either agreed or strongly agreed they learned something from their supervisor, as demonstrated in Figure 4. Figure 5 shows that 95 percent (37) agreed or strongly agreed they learned something from those they supervised during the summer. These results indicate that learning is reciprocal and that individuals are learning from those with more experience, as well as from those with less experience. The results also indicate that supervisors feel strongly that they

Figure 4. Percentage of survey respondents who agreed or strongly agreed with these statements based on the relationship with their supervisor

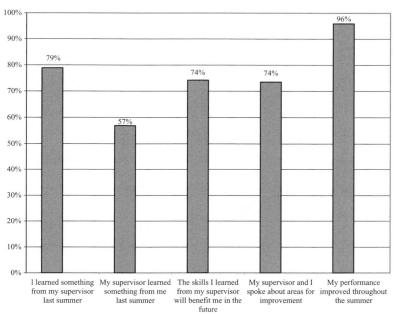

contribute to the development of others and in turn develop their own skills. Individuals are developing their skills not only to improve their immediate performance but also to build skills that will benefit them in the future. Supervisors need to recognize their role as mentors and be intentional about their teaching; however, new participants or employees in an organization should also understand that even those with more experience are learning from them, developing their skills and honing their performance.

The majority of individuals had positive feelings toward their supervisor or those they supervised. Individuals were asked to indicate whether they felt respect, friendship, admiration, connection, or other emotions toward each other. Respondents could select more than one response. Figures 6 and 7 indicate the percentage of respondents who felt the respective feeling toward their supervisor and toward those they supervised, respectfully. Of respondents,

Figure 5. Percentage of survey respondents who agreed or strongly agreed with these statements based on the relationship with those they supervised

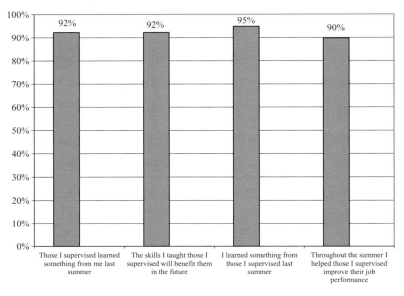

Figure 6. Percentage of survey respondents who agreed with the statements toward their supervisor

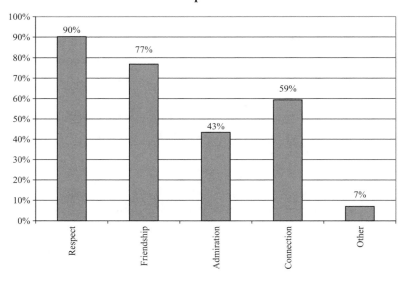

Figure 7. Percentage of survey respondents who agreed with the statements toward those they supervised

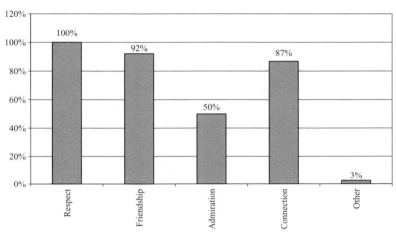

90.2 percent (129) felt respect toward their supervisor; 76.9 percent (110) felt friendship. All who supervised others had at least some positive feeling toward those they supervised.

One hundred percent (38) felt respect toward those they supervised; 92.1 percent (35) felt friendship (Figure 7). The percentages of individuals who felt respect, friendship, admiration, and connection toward each other were relatively high. This foundation of respect and friendship may explain why learning and the development of skills seem so prevalent among CACYS participants. If individuals have high levels of respect and admiration for one another, it seems more likely they will learn from one other and develop their skills for better job performance and for the advancement of their future endeavors.

Discussion and implications

Although CACYS is unique in some respects in comparison with other youth-serving agencies, the results of this study have implications for all organizations, and youth-serving organizations specifically. CACYS recruits and trains college and university students; however, the results of research on these students can be applied to employees of any youth-serving agency. Essentially employees are recruited and trained over some designated period of time and then deliver programs to children and youth. Therefore, for the purposes of discussion and implications, the results of this study can be applied to employees, other youth-serving organizations, and possibly other organizations in general.

This study suggests that all individuals within CACYS were seen as mentors during their training and during program delivery in the summer. The person most likely to be seen as a mentor was the lead trainer. This implies that trainers in youth-serving agencies need to understand their role as a mentor even if this relationship is not formally established. Much of the literature describes this more traditional relationship of those with more experience mentoring those with less experience. When this occurs informally, a person chooses another in an organization with more experience as a mentor without official recognition of the mentor-mentee relationship.[24] Although this often occurs informally, awareness by trainers of their role as mentors may affect their behaviors to be more conducive to a mentoring relationship.

While the lead trainer was most frequently seen as a mentor in this study, it is also important to note that all those in supervisory roles were frequently viewed as mentors as well. This implies that all youth-serving organization supervisors need to understand the importance of their role in advancing the organization's mission and serving children and in developing the competence and effectiveness of youth workers.[25]

One finding that supports the idea of awareness of being a mentor is that 95 percent of respondents felt as though they acted as a mentor specifically toward a counselor. This may indicate that while these mentoring relationships are informal, those with more experience in the organization recognize their role as a mentor to new employees. Being intentional about one's actions as a mentor may prove to be beneficial for those in the mentoring relationship and the organization as a whole. If individuals are aware that others are looking to them as role models, they may take steps to nurture the mentoring relationship to improve the quality of new employees' performance, enhance motivation and learning, and demonstrate organizational values.[26] It is important to note that all youth workers, supervisors, and administrators in youth-serving organizations are likely to be seen as mentors.

The results of this study not only indicate the existence of mentoring relationships, but also highlight that individuals learn from their supervisor and those in supervisory roles also learn from those they supervise. This finding supports the two vital components recognized by some researchers as necessary in mentoring relationships: reciprocity and the willingness of each party in the relationship to grow and change.[27] Analyses of the results seem to suggest that mentoring helps students or employees better understand the organization. Mentoring appears to help participants understand what is expected of them and how they can succeed in the organization during training and summer implementation. Given the learning that is occurring as a result of informal mentoring relationships, youth-serving organizations appear to recognize this opportunity and intentionally develop a mentoring program to enhance performance.

One key to mentoring seems to be the presence of individuals who can share experiences with new participants as they arrive at the organization; however, an interesting finding not explored in the literature is that 95 percent of respondents indicated they had learned something from those they supervised. Respondents who are in a supervisory role in CACYS are likely to be experienced and would equate to employees who have been with an organization for some time.

One exciting aspect of this learning is that it creates the potential for the continuous development and growth of all participants, including those who are more experienced. Even those who have been in the organization for years look to others in the organization, including their subordinates, for support and guidance. Individuals have the potential to keep growing and honing their abilities as they work to teach others. Youth-serving organizations need to work to develop the opportunity for continued development for the leaders in their organization in order to retain these individuals.

Another important implication of this study is that students believe that the skills they developed will assist them not only in future participation in the CACYS program but also in other future endeavors. Youth-serving organizations need to recognize the learning and improvement in performance that results from mentoring relationships. These organizations should continue, or begin, to emphasize the opportunity employees have to develop or improve their skills and abilities to enhance their personal growth. Prospective employees would seemingly be attracted to the opportunity to enhance their personal growth and develop their skills and abilities in their work in a particular youth-serving organization and in their future career.

An encouraging result of this research shows that individuals are very likely to respect, develop friendship with, admire, and build a connection with their supervisor, and leaders have these same feelings toward those they supervise. All supervisors felt respect toward those they supervised, and 90 percent of the respondents respected their supervisor. Admiration and connection were least indicated, while showing respect and friendship were both highly indicated and seem to be present for both parties in the mentoring relationship. These results indicate that youth-serving organizations have a place of respect and friendship from which to build mentoring relationships.

One aspect important to engaging in a formal mentoring relationship is the willingness to learn from one another and grow as a result, and it seems as though staff who respect and feel friendship toward one another are more willing to engage in a mentoring relationship. Organizations that find a sense of respect and friendship between and among staff may have a foundation from which to build a mentoring program.

This study indicates that mentoring relationships do exist between new and experienced staff; therefore, it might be beneficial for youth-serving organizations to program or schedule informal time for new staff to interact with more experienced staff. While mentoring and learning may happen on the job, "storytelling" and other "lessons-learned" conversations can be crafted during meetings and other activities so that relationships can be developed for the benefit of individuals as well as the organization.

Finally, although mentoring can occur informally, a further recommendation is that youth-serving organizations develop formal mentoring programs for staff members. Administrators may pair a new employee with an experienced employee both on the job and during informal time. While the benefits of mentoring relationships may just "happen," it may be even more beneficial to structure a program and have the benefits of mentoring be realized in an intentional manner so as to create the most positive and rewarding environment possible. Research, as well as the results of this study, indicate that mentoring does benefit individuals but is also beneficial to the organization. As a result, developing a mentoring program with intentional efforts to develop an individual's skills will have positive effects on the program as a whole.

Future research

Perhaps one of the most exciting aspects of this research is that it provides the foundation for further research related to mentoring in youth-serving organizations. One point to consider is that if mentoring relationships are so prevalent among staff who are working with children and youth, further research needs to be conducted about the mentoring occurring between the youth worker and the youth themselves. Of utmost importance is gaining an understanding of how those relationships are formed, affect youth, and affect youth workers. While this area of research has been explored, there is more to learn about the implications of mentoring on youth specifically.

More research is necessary to understand how to increase the capacity for organizations to promote mentoring among staff. By understanding how mentoring relationships are happening with or without intentional efforts on the part of supervisors and administrators, the study of intentional efforts to foster healthy mentoring programs will assist youth-serving organizations in developing, promoting, and organizing mentoring relationships that will benefit those in the mentoring relationships as well as the organization.

Conclusion

We set out to understand how mentoring within a particular youth-serving organization contributes to the development of its participants during their training and the delivery of the program. Mentoring relationships were taking place in both the staff development program and during delivery of the program in the summer as students worked to develop their own skills and abilities and understand the complex culture of CACYS.

The mentoring that took place during the staff development program requires the more experienced staff of the program to use their leadership and experience to support and comfort new participants and teach them the skills necessary to find success in CACYS. During the summer, more experienced program participants mentor newer participants as they work to support them in the complex summer experience.

The results of this study are meaningful not only for CACYS but for other youth-serving organizations. Many of these organizations must find ways to support new participants as they learn more about the culture of the organization. Mentoring is an effective way to support individuals new to the organization while allowing others in the organization to continue developing their own leadership and confidence through acting as mentors for newer staff. Supervisors and administrators of youth-serving organizations should be intentional about developing and promoting healthy mentoring relationships to create positive environments for staff and the youth being served.

NEW DIRECTIONS FOR YOUTH DEVELOPMENT • DOI: 10.1002/yd

Notes

1. Hale, M. (1996). Learning organizations and mentoring: Two ways to link learning and workforce development. *Public Productivity and Management Review, 19*(4), 422–433.

2. Thach, E., & Thompson, K. (2007). Trading places: Examining leadership competencies between for-profit vs. public and non-profit leaders. *Leadership and Organization Development Journal, 28*(4), 356–375.

3. Launer, J. (2010). Supervision, mentoring, and coaching. In T. Swanwick (Ed.), *Understanding medical education: Evidence, theory and practice.* (pp. 111-123). Hoboken, NJ: Wiley-Blackwell.

4. Thach & Thompson. (2007).

5. Launer. (2010).

6. Turner, B. (2000). Supervision and mentoring in child and family social work: The role of the first-line manager in the implementation of the post-qualifying framework. *Social Work Education, 19*(3), 231–240.

7. Hale. (1996).

8. Healy, C., & Welchert, A. (1990). Mentoring relations: A definition to advance research and practice. *Educational Researcher, 19*(9), 17–21.

9. Healy & Welchert. (1990).

10. Hale. (1966).

11. Healy & Welchert. (1990). P. 17.

12. Bryant, S. (2005). The impact of peer mentoring on organizational knowledge creation and sharing. *Group and Organization Management, 30*(3), 319–338.

13. Bryant. (2005).

14. O'Neill, R. (2005). An examination of organizational predictors of mentoring functions. *Journal of Managerial Issues, 17*(4), 439–462.

15. Hale. (1966).

16. Godshalk, V., & Sosik, J. (2000). Leadership styles, mentoring function received, and job-related stress: A conceptual model and preliminary study. *Journal of Organizational Behavior, 21*(4), 365–390.

17. Fullan, M., & Hargreaves, A. (2000). Mentoring in the new millennium. *Theory into Practice, 39*(1), 50–56.

18. Hale. (1966).

19. Bryant. (2005).

20. Matthews, P. (2006). The role of mentoring in promoting organizational competitiveness. *Competitiveness Review: An International Business Journal incorporating Journal of Global Competitiveness, 16*(2), 158–169.

21. Godshalk & Sosik. (2000).

22. O'Neill. (2005).

23. Allen, T., Eby, L., & Lentz, E. (2006). Mentoring behaviors and mentorship quality associated with formal mentoring programs: Closing the gap between research and practice. *Journal of Applied Psychology, 91*(3), 567–578.

24. Bryant. (2005).

25. O'Neill. (2005).

26. Hale. (1966).
27. Healy & Welchert. (1990).

JULIANNE GASSMAN *is an assistant professor in the School of Health, Physical Education and Leisure Services at the University of Northern Iowa; executive director of the Nonprofit Leadership Alliance; and associate director of Camp Adventure Child and Youth Services.*

MICHAEL C. GLEASON *is the associate for Vocation and Mentoring in the Pathways Center of Wartburg College in Waverly, Iowa. He also serves as director of the High School Leadership Institute and as a fellow and instructor in the Institute for Leadership Education.*

Putting youth development into practice: Learning from an innovative fellowship program

Robert L. Fischer, Monica A. G. Craven, Patricia Heilbron

Abstract

Professionals who work with youth can have a tremendous impact on the development and life trajectory of these young people. This article reports on an effort to provide support and professional development for those who work with youth during nonschool hours in a youth development fellowship program. Combining intensive residency workshops and a six-month coaching experience, the fellowship was designed to teach participants how to integrate youth resilience and youth development perspectives into their work. The evaluation collected data from the fellows and their coaches during the course of the program. The study offers insights into the types of benefits achieved through this type of focused intervention with youth workers, as well as the challenges of conducting such an effort.

PROFESSIONALS WORKING WITH youth can have a tremendous impact on the development and life trajectory of young people. These professionals come from varied backgrounds and possess a range of skill sets and experience that leads to tremendous variability within the profession. The advent of positive youth development and resilience frameworks has led to productive advances within the youth-serving sector. Yet these concepts are not uniformly in use among youth workers.

This study was made possible through support from the Treu-Mart Fund. We thank all the fellows and coaches who participated in this study.

NEW DIRECTIONS FOR YOUTH DEVELOPMENT, SUPPLEMENT 2011 © WILEY PERIODICALS, INC.
Published online in Wiley Online Library (wileyonlinelibrary.com) • DOI: 10.1002/yd.420

This article reports on one community's efforts to provide support and professional development for those who work with youth during nonschool hours. The youth development fellowship program examined here was developed and implemented in 2005–2006, and data are presented on the first three cohorts of participants ($N = 45$). Delivered in a set of intensive residency workshops and a six-month coaching experience, the fellowship sought to teach participants how to integrate youth resilience and youth development perspectives into their work. The evaluation collected data from the fellows throughout the experience, as well as from coaches after the program. The study offers insights into the benefits achieved through this type of focused intervention with youth workers, as well as the challenges of conducting such an effort.

Background

In the past two decades, there has been increasing focus on the use of youth resilience and youth development perspectives. This view and the accompanying research emerged from academic circles and expanded dramatically over time across professional and practice environments.[1] Positive youth development is now seen as complementary to the discipline of prevention science.[2] Despite this convergence, the practical issue of embedding youth development and resilience constructs within community-based youth programming has remained challenging. In specific, mechanisms for developing the necessary competencies in youth development within the cadre of youth service workers have been a topic of great interest.[3]

Although postsecondary approaches to this issue are viable for many future professionals, there is wide acknowledgment of the need for a diversity of professional development strategies.[4] The fundamental acknowledgment of youth development as a field of work and a profession whose elements can be described is still a relatively recent proposition.[5] This, along with the issues facing youth professionals in the field, has led to haphazard emphasis on the promotion of youth development among community-based youth service workers.[6] Furthermore, very few examples of program models with this intent are described in the literature, and even fewer have been subjected to systematic evaluation.

Program context

This study describes the development, implementation, and initial outcomes of a pilot fellowship program for youth service workers.[7] The model underlying the design of the fellowship is grounded in a strong theoretical base and is tied to evidence about how to effectively communicate this information to youth workers. The model was developed with the intention of producing three types of change in program staff: changes in thinking, in mode of relating, and in the way individuals view the role of community-based organizations in the lives of youth.

To guide the study effort, key stakeholders were convened in early 2005 to flesh out the goals of the project and the evaluation plan. Figure 1 provides the logic model for the fellowship program as developed during that process. The model clearly shows how the developers envisioned the fellowship experience would lead to changes in the youth service workers, which will ultimately have a positive impact on the lives of the children with whom they work. The fellowship experience was configured as three residency events over six days, where the fellows came together for a learning experience. Following the residency phase was a six-month peer support and coaching period. All of these aspects of the program were conducted in metropolitan Cleveland, Ohio.

The model for the Treu-Mart Youth Development Fellowship was developed through collaboration between the Mandel Center for Nonprofit Organizations and the Treu-Mart Fund, including participation by community agency staff and national advisors. The model that emerged has three elements: educational experience, peer support and reinforcement, and coaching.

NEW DIRECTIONS FOR YOUTH DEVELOPMENT • DOI: 10.1002/yd

Figure 1. Logic model for Treu-Mart Youth Development Fellowship Program

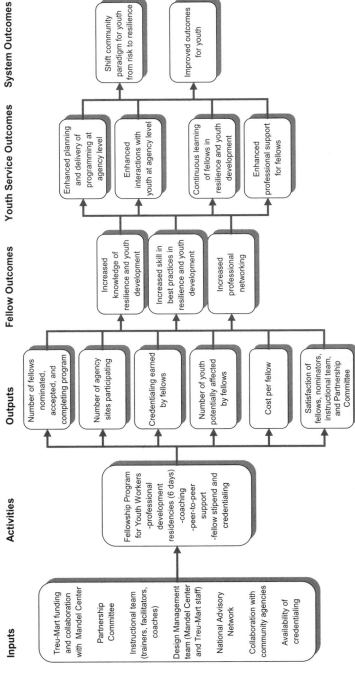

Educational experience

The first program component offered three residencies approximately one month apart that combine a nontraditional participatory educational experience with opportunities for fellows to internalize the concepts of resilience—that is, to help the participants themselves become more resilient. Youth development concepts and best practices were woven into a framework of resilience, integrating theory and practice.

Peer support and reinforcement

The second component provides a follow-up process that supports and reinforces resilience and youth development concepts. Based on the concepts established by the center's successful Leaders Links program, groups of five to ten participants met once a month for facilitated conversations about their experiences in integrating the resilience model and positive youth development into their daily work. Applicants to the fellowship program repeatedly spoke of the need for this type of peer support in both their applications and interviews, reinforcing the earlier belief that peer support is a critical need for youth development professionals.

Coaching

The third component provided one-to-one coaching and feedback to assist fellows to successfully implement concepts of resilience and youth development in their work with youth. This component is critical to fellows as they face barriers when working to modify personal and organizational practice as well as organizational culture.

Methodology

The pilot study focused on two primary questions: Was the fellowship implemented in a manner that was appropriate to the needs of the fellows? and Did the fellowship experience lead to benefits for the participants in regard to increased knowledge and application

NEW DIRECTIONS FOR YOUTH DEVELOPMENT • DOI: 10.1002/yd

of best practices in resilience and youth development and use of professional networking? The study employed an observational design based on data provided by the individuals in the fellowship experience.

Participants were asked to provide data on the implementation, content, and impact of the fellowship experience during the course of a nine-month period. Data were collected in two fashions. First, detailed surveys were used at baseline, the postresidency phase, and six-month follow-up to examine trends over time and gauge participants' perceptions of the experience. In addition, for the second and third cohorts, coaches were surveyed after the six-month coaching phase. Second, participant feedback was collected from brief written instruments administered at the end of each of the three residencies. The postresidency feedback forms were designed to collect focused feedback on the content and delivery of each of the residencies. Evaluation instruments were developed specifically for this project and were made available to the sponsor prior to use for comment.

Results

The evaluation of the delivery of the fellowship experience is examined in two ways. In regard to the implementation of the fellowship, process data were collected according to the program logic model. In addition, outcome-oriented data were collected at three points: baseline, postresidency phase, and follow-up.

Fellow profile

The demographic profile of the three cohorts is presented in Table 1. Across the three cohorts the participants were predominantly female (73.3 percent) and African American (68.9 percent). The average age for all cohorts was 34.9, with a range from 23 to 53. Nearly all of the fellows had completed high school (95.6 percent), and two-thirds had a college degree (68.9 percent). In addition, 33.3 percent had a postgraduate degree.

NEW DIRECTIONS FOR YOUTH DEVELOPMENT • DOI: 10.1002/yd

Table 1. Fellow profile

	Cohort 1	*Cohort 2*	*Cohort 3*	*Total*
Number of fellows	16	14	15	45
Gender				
Female	81.3%	64.3%	73.3%	73.3%
Male	18.8%	42.9%	25.0%	26.7%
Race				
African American	50.0%	85.7%	73.3%	68.9%
White	50.0%	14.3%	26.7%	31.1%
Age				
Average age	33.3	34.7	36.9	34.9
Age range	26-53	23-52	27-53	23-53
Age 20-29	43.8%	28.6%	26.7%	33.3%
Age 30-39	31.3%	50.0%	40.0%	40.0%
Educational attainment				
Completed high school	93.7%	100.0%	93.3%	95.6%
Some college	93.7%	85.7%	93.3%	91.2%
College degree	75.0%	50.0%	80.0%	68.9%
Postgraduate degree	43.8%	21.4%	33.3%	33.3%

Process data

The fellowship guidelines required that each fellow be nominated and submit an application. Some individuals were unable to enroll in the fellowship, and others were unable to complete the program for personal reasons. Each cohort had varying numbers at each of these stages (Table 2).

Fellows were nominated and represented the agency where they work, and in some cases individuals from the same agency were both nominated and selected. Fellows had the option of receiving continuing education credits for the fellowship if they so desired. The number of youth who are touched by a cohort is estimated based on service data showing that fellows work with forty youth per year on average. The average cost of delivering the fellowship is approximated by dividing the total cost by the number of participants. The costs (presented in 2006 dollars) include program personnel, evaluation, general expense (materials, marketing,

Table 2. Program process data

	Cohort 1	Cohort 2	Cohort 3	Total
Number nominated	29	22	32	83
Number applied	26	18	20	64
Number accepted	17	16	15	48
Number participated	16	15	15	46
Number completed	16	14	14	44
Number of agencies of nominees	20	19	29	68
Number of agencies of participants	12	15	14	41
Number receiving continuing education credits	4	8	7	19
Youth affected each year	640	560	560	1,760
Cost per fellow	$13,889	$13,609	$13,609	$13,702
Satisfaction, residency 1	100.0%	99.0%	99.0%	99.4%
Satisfaction, residency 2	94.0%	99.0%	98.0%	99.9%
Satisfaction, residency 3	87.0%	100.0%	99.0%	95.0%

phone, and similar expenses), the nomination process, residency costs, coaching, peer session, stipend, and training cost for consultant staff.

The satisfaction of the participants was assessed continuously, including after each of the residency components and in the evaluation forms after the residency phase and at follow-up. Table 2 summarizes the fellows' ratings of the residency experience and generally shows high levels of satisfaction. Of note is the relatively low satisfaction for the third residency in comparison to the previous two residencies. The low ratings given by the first cohort resulted in program curriculum changes, and higher scores from the subsequent cohorts are evident. The figures suggest an overall sense of satisfaction since most categories were ranked "strongly agree" by 80 percent of fellows. Also the number of fellows who selected "agree" on the satisfaction scale makes up almost all of the remainder in more than half of the categories for each residency.

Outcome data

A key focus of this work was on the overall experience of the participants by examining their feedback after the residency phase and then at the six-month follow-up point. In addition, some elements are examined longitudinally from baseline to postresidency to follow-up.

Personal resilience. One method of increasing knowledge and understanding of the importance of resilience within the youth development perspective is to increase the personal knowledge and awareness of the youth workers of their own personal resilience. To capture this dimension, a fifteen-point scale tapping a number of aspects of personal resilience was used. Each item consists of a statement that reflects an aspect of positive personal resilience. Respondents were asked to indicate their level of personal agreement with each statement on a five-point Likert scale, ranging from *strongly disagree* (1) to *strongly agree* (5). The total value of the scale ranged from fifteen to seventy-five. The scale was also divided into four subscales based on the constructs of supportive personal resources, positive sense of self, positive and supportive work environment, and personal skills.

The overall change in the mean score of the resilience scale from baseline (M = 63.0) to follow-up (M = 64.5) was small, registering just over a one-point increase on the scale. Similarly, the four subscales (supportive personal resources, positive sense of self, personal skills, and positive and supportive work environment) had mean differences of less than 1 point. A paired t-test showed no statistical significance between the baseline values and either the postresidency or six-month values for any of the five resilience scales. It is possible that changes on these dimensions may not be detectable during this short time frame.

Analysis of the individual items in the scale does suggest that some changes occurred over the course of the youth development fellowship program. Three items in particular showed a large increase in the number of respondents who strongly agreed with the statement. Item 3 ("I take time to nurture myself"), item 5 ("I get the message 'you can succeed at work'"), and item 14 ("I have skills to do my job well") all increased by half or more in the number of strong positive responses provided. Item 14 suggests that fellows felt they had tangible increases in skills and confidence to fulfill their work responsibilities.

Overall helpfulness of the program. As a means of providing feedback on the components of the program, respondents were asked to rate seven program components using a helpfulness scale ranging from *very helpful* to *not helpful*). When completing the six-month follow-up survey, the fellows were asked to indicate the level of helpfulness during the preceding six-month period (see Figure 2). The most highly rated elements were the strategies and theories learned during the residencies. with *very helpful* ratings of 81.0 percent and 73.8 percent, respectively. Materials and resources given out were also highly rated at 71.4 percent indicating *very helpful*. Approximately two-thirds of the fellows rated the consultation from their coach as *very helpful*. Interaction with other fellowship staff and networking were rated as *very helpful* by just over half and were *moderately helpful* by an additional

NEW DIRECTIONS FOR YOUTH DEVELOPMENT • DOI: 10.1002/yd

Figure 2. Fellow ratings of the helpfulness of program aspects during postresidency phase

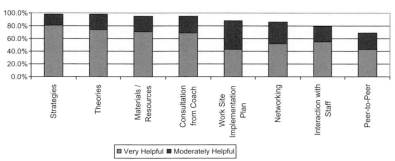

26 to 33 percent Finally, although work site implementation plans and peer-to-peer sessions were rated as *very helpful* by just under half of the fellows, an additional 26 to 46 percent rated them as *moderately helpful.*

Importance and effectiveness on the job. One of the desired outcomes of the program was to increase the fellows' knowledge of youth development and to enhance their ability to apply this knowledge in the workplace. Overall, fellows reported less achievement of high effectiveness compared to the proportion reporting that the content was of high importance in their job. Four areas were particularly divergent. Building relationships with youth, creating meaningful opportunities for youth participation in program delivery, and networking with other professionals in youth services had substantial gaps between the percentage who felt the skill was highly important and the percentage who felt they were highly effective in using the skill. Fellows noted that they were very highly successful in implementing the resilience perspective in program delivery in a greater proportion than those who highly valued the importance of this in their work. This indicates they were more successful with this new skill in their work setting than they had anticipated.

Fellow outcomes. The key outcomes sought for the fellows were increased knowledge of resilience and youth development, increased skill in applying best practices in resilience and youth development, and increased professional networking. Each of these outcomes is addressed in turn.

Knowledge of resilience and youth development. When fellows were asked in the follow-up period about the helpfulness of the strategies they learned during the residencies, 81.0 percent stated that the strategies were *very helpful*, and an additional 16.7 percent stated the strategies were *moderately helpful*. When asked a similar question about the theories learned during the residencies, 73.8 percent stated the theories were *very helpful*, and an additional 23.8 percent indicated the strategies were *moderately helpful*.

Knowledge of resilience and the application of resilience theory to work with youth was the most commonly identified example of knowledge that fellows stated they took away from the residency experience. One fellow identified the exposure to resilience theory as the most important aspect of the fellowship. Also, several fellows noted the importance of how they interact with youth as being particularly useful knowledge they gained through the residency. Fellows specifically stated that they learned how they should be more aware of the behavior of the youth and the importance of patience when working with these young people and how youth tend to have different coping skills that may help to explain some of their behaviors. In regard to skill development, one fellow wrote:

I think constantly focusing on what the kids are doing right instead of what needs to be fixed has made a huge difference in how I interact with the kids on a daily basis. Much of our paperwork, curriculum, and how much participation and ownership we share with the kids has all been improved. We were doing bits and pieces of resilience, but really needed the overarching structure or unifying philosophy of resilience to bring it all together.

In addition, the ability to connect and network with other fellows and to value their own resilience were seen as an important opportunities and resources. In regard to skills taken away, one fellow wrote:

I really enjoyed the camaraderie, and the opportunity to truly witness and experience professional development at its best. This personal experience has encouraged me to continue to develop youth programming in a format that requires youth to take active roles in the programs they are asked to participate in.

Skill in applying best practices. The second outcome sought for the fellows was to increase skill in applying best practices in resilience and youth development. The best measures of this dimension come from data collected at follow-up in which the fellows were asked to rate the importance of strategies in their work and their effectiveness in using these strategies. In addition, fellows identified new perspectives and skills they acquired through the fellowship.

The fellows identified a wide range of new perspectives, including helpful insights on problem solving, relating to staff and youth, being more positive in their outlook, and being more mindful of interpersonal connections. Fellows specifically noted the value of the experience:

It's had a major effect on the way I do things. In carrying out my plan, I explain the concepts of resilience to the kids, and seeing just how they respond to the changes has motivated me to do things at a bigger level. I am working with our regional director to develop a resilience director position for me because it's been so positive.

Several fellows indicated that the residency helped them develop a new perspective on problem solving. One fellow now "looks for the 'gift' in the problem." Another fellow referred to a new perspective "that problems are an opportunity to creatively solve a challenge."

Perhaps the most helpful aspect that the program fellows identified was the importance of taking a strengths-based or a positive youth development approach in working with the youth. One fellow now focuses on "what the kids are doing right" as opposed to a traditional deficit-based approach, and another mentioned looking "at the teen's strengths." Yet another has learned to pause and attempt to "understand why children do the things they do" before reacting. Finally, one fellow, after completing the residency, now recognizes that youth truly want programming focused on principles of youth development and resilience. One described the program experience in this way:

I think this has been a tremendously positive experience. It is not the kind of workshop experience where momentum is lost the minute you walk out the door. The knowledge and skills learned will stay with me. I have made significant changes to our program structurally and how we, as adults, work with youth on a day-to-day basis.

The theme of increased confidence and self-belief emerged across a range of comments, suggesting that the fellowship produced a greater sense of control for participants. This strength may be particularly important given the volatility in the field and the likelihood that fellows' home agency policies may not be explicitly supportive of resilience-based programming efforts.

Professional networks. The third outcome identified for the youth development fellows was an increase in professional networks. This was evident in their greater collaboration with other fellows and other youth development colleagues and in networking within the youth services profession. At the six-month follow-up point, fellows were asked to report on the helpfulness of networking with the other fellows during this follow-up period: 52 percent stated that networking with other fellows was *very helpful* and another 33 percent that it was *moderately helpful*. Fellows commented on the benefit of connection to others in the field:

Meeting a large group of resilient, passionate people, in the same field as I, was very influential to my well being. Being at the same agency for [many] years has isolated me to this work experience. It has given me new energy to carry on what I do, enforced what I do well, and given me new ideas to present to the agency.

Fellows described the opportunity as "taking their ideas and making them work for my organization" and "creating meaningful relationships for me that now extend far beyond the ending of the fellowship." These connections have the potential to result in lasting bonds among professionals that will live well beyond the fellowship experience. To the extent that these professionals can provide ongoing support and encouragement to each other, the overall effect of the experience is compounded.

Fellows were asked how well the content of the residency experience would translate back into their current work environment, specifically collaborating and networking with other professionals in youth services. The fellows were asked to indicate how important these two factors were going to be in their work and how effective they felt they would be at using these content areas. At the six-month follow-up, the fellows were again asked how important each aspect was in their work and to indicate how effective they felt they had been in each area over the preceding six months. In regard to professional collaboration, approximately two-thirds of fellows reported at the end of the residency phase that this would be important in their work, and almost 70 percent estimated that they would be effective in using the strategies. After six months, only 50 percent had found the strategy highly important in their job, and less than a third reported a high level of effectiveness in the use of the approach. In regard to professional networking, two-thirds of fellows reported at the end of the residency phase that this would be important in their work and that they would be effective in using the strategies. After six months, a similar percentage, 65 percent, found the strategy highly important in their job, but less than half reported effectiveness in the use of the approach. These lower ratings of effectiveness speak to the challenges of implementing change in an organizational practice environment.

Youth services outcomes

The key outcomes sought for fellows in the arena of youth services were better service planning and delivery, interactions with youth

NEW DIRECTIONS FOR YOUTH DEVELOPMENT • DOI: 10.1002/yd

that better reflect resiliency principles, continuous learning of fellows, and increased professional support for fellows. Each of these outcomes is addressed in turn.

Planning and delivery of programming

The planning component includes measures of youth development and youth resilience perspectives, and the delivery of programming focuses on meaningful opportunities and decision making. At the end of the residency phase, fellows were asked specifically about drawing on the resilience perspective and the youth development perspective in planning programming for youth. They were asked to indicate how important these factors were going to be in their work and how effective they felt they would be at using these skills.

Overall, participants felt these perspectives were important, and most felt they were effective in incorporating these perspectives in the planning of youth services. In regard to drawing on the resilience perspective in planning, nearly all fellows reported at the end of the residency phase that this would be important in their work, and three-quarters reported that they would be effective in using the strategy. After six months, four-fifths still found the strategy highly important in their job, and three-quarters reported being highly effective in the use of the approach. In regard to drawing on a youth development perspective in planning, four-fifths of fellows reported at the end of the residency phase that this would be important in their work, and two-thirds reported that they would be effective in using the strategy. After six months, three-quarters had found the strategy highly important in their job, and just over half reported being highly effective in the use of the approach.

In addition, fellows were asked about involving youth in decision making and creating opportunities for participation in the delivery of youth programming. Overall, participants felt these aspects of programming were quite important, with creating opportunities for meaningful participation having the most respondents stating it was of high importance. In regard to

NEW DIRECTIONS FOR YOUTH DEVELOPMENT • DOI: 10.1002/yd

involving youth in decision making, nearly all fellows reported at the end of the residency phase that this would be important in their work, but only three-quarters still thought this after six months. Two-thirds felt they would be effective in using this strategy, and the same percentage found that they were effective in using the approach after six months. In regard to creating opportunities for meaningful participation of youth, nearly all of the fellows reported at the end of the residency phase that this would be important in their work, and three-fourths believed they would be effective in using the strategy. After six months, the proportion who found the strategy highly important in their job had stayed the same, while those who felt they were highly effective in the use of the approach had declined to two-thirds.

Interactions with youth

Overall, fellows indicated this content area was very important and that they felt somewhat effective in using this skill area. In regard to building relationships with youth, four-fifths of fellows reported at the end of the residency phase that this would be important in their work, and three-quarters expected that they would be effective in using the strategy. After six months, four-fifths had found the strategy highly important in their job, but only slightly less than two-thirds were indeed highly effective in the use of the approach. In regard to understanding and dealing with conflict, just two-thirds of fellows reported at the end of the residency phase that this would be important in their work, and just over half expected to be effective in using the strategies. After six months, the percentages remained the same.

Continuous learning of fellows

A primary quantitative measure looks at the use of the work site implementation plans that were designed as a part of the residencies. In the six-month follow-up survey, fellows were asked to indicate how helpful the development of a personalized work site implementation plan had been in the postresidency period. Responses were positive, with 42.9 percent of fellows indicating the plans were *very helpful*, and another 45.2 percent reporting the plan was *moderately helpful*.

Professional support for fellows

Professional support refers to the peer-to-peer learning that was incorporated in the postresidency phase and the consultation from the coaches who worked with the fellows during the six-month follow-up period. Peer-to-peer learning was captured by fellow ratings of the helpfulness of the peer-to-peer learning sessions during the postresidency period. Of the forty-two respondents, 42.9 percent (eighteen fellows) stated that the sessions were very helpful, and 26.2 percent of respondents stated moderately helpful. Another measure focused on the peer-to-peer learning and how effective the fellows felt they had been in using this aspect of the program. When asked how satisfied they were with the peer-to-peer sessions, 36.0 percent of fellows rated the experience as a 7 on a seven-point scale (completely satisfied), and 28.0 percent rated it as a 6. Fewer fellows (24.0 percent) rated the experience in the moderate range (3 to 5 on seven-point scale) and 12.0 percent in the low range (1 or 2 on the scale).

In the six-month follow-up survey, fellows were asked to indicate how helpful the consultation with their coach had been during the preceding six months. When asked how satisfied they were with the coaching experience, 56.0 percent of fellows rated the experience as a 7 on a seven-point scale, with an additional 12.0 percent rating it a 6. On the seven-point scale, 24.0 percent rated the experience in the moderate range (3 to 5), and 8.0 percent rated it in the low range (1 or 2 on the scale). Of note is that six of the eight moderate and low rankings came from the second cohort. The areas in which fellows reported the largest improvements due to the coaching experience were growth as a youth professional (57.7 percent), leadership skills/confidence (53.8 percent), and application of the concepts of resilience (56.0 percent). In their narrative comments, fellows cited coaches' flexibility, openness, professionalism, and encouragement as key attributes of the experience. In regard to problem areas, fellows reported insufficient time with or scheduling problems with their coach. Fellows reported that the coaching interaction extended far beyond the fellowship content:

The fact that I had my own coach during this time gave me a feeling of pride. When I said to people, "I have to go meet my coach," they were impressed. I had the chance to stick out my chest from a professional standpoint, I was able to relate on a one-on-one level. She was there to listen to me and guide me in the right direction.

The most frequent benefit that the fellows cited was the coach as a sounding board, where the coach helped the fellow to problem-solve, think creatively, or, on some occasions, just vent. Several fellows felt the biggest impact of the coach was that it reaffirmed what they were already doing or already knew. The coach supported the use of resources, materials, and approaches that the fellows were already implementing as a result of the residencies. Another common theme was that the coaches promoted a solutions-focused approach.

In comparing the fellows' ratings of the importance of various elements to their work and their own effectiveness in using strategies during the postresidency phase, several interesting findings emerge. Table 3 presents the strategies according to the proportion reporting that the strategy was highly important and whether they had been highly effective in its use. In the matrix, "higher" represents ratings of 75 percent and above, "lower" refers to ratings 50 percent and below, and "moderate" refers to ratings in between.

Among the strategies that fellows found to be highly important in their work, they report high effectiveness for one strategy and moderate effectiveness for three others. For strategies they rated as being of moderate importance in their work, the fellows reported moderate effectiveness for three strategies and lower effectiveness for two others. Only one strategy was rated as low in importance and effectiveness. This pattern indicates some success in translating the fellowship content back into their work

Table 3. Importance of and effectiveness in use of strategies during postresidency period

Effectiveness in use of strategy during postresidency period	Importance of strategy in their work during the postresidency period		
	Higher importance	*Moderate importance*	*Lower importance*
Higher effectiveness	Drawing on resilience perspective in planning programming		
Moderate effectiveness	Involving youth in decision making Building relationships with youth Creating meaningful opportunities for participation of youth	Drawing on youth development perspective in planning programming Drawing on resilience perspective in planning program delivery Understanding and dealing with conflict	
Lower effectiveness		Drawing on youth development perspective in program delivery Networking with other professionals in youth services	Collaborating with fellows and other colleagues

environment but also suggests that to the extent that fellows perceive some strategies as less important in their work, this correlates to their effectiveness in the use of those strategies. This is demonstrated in Table 4, which presents the statistical significance between the postresidency data and the six-month follow-up. The table shows that three categories (resilience perspective in planning, youth development in planning, and involving youth in decision making) became significantly less important over this time period. In addition, two categories (collaborating with fellows and other colleagues and networking with other professionals in youth services) showed significantly less effectiveness than fellows originally anticipated. These data reemphasize the dichotomy between the classroom experience and real-world application.

Coach feedback

Over the six-month period, coaches reported having an average of eight face-to-face meetings with fellows, totaling some twelve hours. The majority (58 percent) felt this amount was just right, but an additional 39 percent thought it was too little. Coaches also reported phone contact (less than two hours) and e-mail communication (one hour) over the coaching period, amounts that more than 80 percent of coaches deemed sufficient.

Coaches were asked to explicitly address things that did and did not work well in their coaching relationship. Narrative responses included a wide range of comments. (Throughout the quotations that follow, the fellows are referred to using the feminine pronoun regardless of gender.) In regard to aspects of the coaching that worked well, coaches highlighted the importance of fellows being open to suggestions and new ideas (that is, being coachable)—for example:

[The fellow] and I got along well, and she was willing to try new things. I think that the fellowship caused her to rethink her profession—whether or not she sees what she does as work or a career and she began to lean

Table 4. Importance and effectiveness of programmatic elements at postresidency and six-month follow-up

	Importance			Effectiveness		
	Postresidency	Six-Month Follow-up	p-Value	Postresidency	Six-month follow-up	p-Value
Resilience perspective in planning	92.9%	82.5%	0.096*	71.4%	75.0%	0.564
Youth development in planning	85.4	74.4	0.034**	65.9	58.3	0.197
Building relationships with youth	88.1	87.5	0.763	73.8	62.2	0.142
Involving youth in decision making	85.7	75.0	0.096*	61.9	62.2	0.251
Creating opportunities for meaningful youth participation	88.1	87.5	0.739	76.2	67.6	0.225
Understanding and dealing with conflict	66.7	66.7	0.224	54.8	54.1	0.627
Collaborating with fellows and other colleagues	61.9	50.0	0.248	69.0	32.4	0.000***
Networking with other professionals in youth services	61.9	65.0	1.000	61.9	40.5	0.046**

*Significant at .10 level. ** Significant at .05 level. *** Significant at .01 level.

more toward career. She shared this as well as her apprehension about going back to school, if in fact she will make that choice.

Coaches also noted the value of fellows being proactive in coaching relationship—for example:

[The fellow] took advantage of coaching sessions by bringing issues to the table. Although few were global issues, she is getting better at looking at the big picture. She now can more clearly see her own strengths; knows what she is good at and enjoys. She has learned that she does not want to be in a supervisory role as she was earlier this year.

In regard to aspects of the coaching that did not work well, coaches also noted a number of themes. They identified difficulties in carving out time for coaching and making the most of the time that had been established—for example:

[The fellow] was very evasive and defensive in making comments about her project. When questioned about her progress, she always had excuses for her lack of program completion and lack of written documentation she had been asked to provide as evidence of her project completion.

One challenging issue manifested itself in trying to coordinate our schedules. We were both very busy, which at times presented various challenges. However, we managed to work through this problem.

Coaches also expressed concern about the plans that the fellows developed and the support that they received at their work sites—for example:

Multiple demands on her life personally and professionally made it challenging to connect. I am not sure she really knew how to take advantage of the benefit of having a coach in her life. In her case, the peer-to-peer meetings seemed to be more beneficial.

A final point involved the coaches' satisfaction with their involvement in the experience. When asked how satisfied they

were with the coaching experience, nearly two-thirds (70.3 percent) rated the experience as a 6 or 7 on a seven-point scale. An
additional 18.5 percent rated the experience as a 4 or 5, and the
remaining 11.1 percent ranked it as a 2 or 3. The areas in which
coaches reported the largest fellow improvements due to the
coaching experience were leadership skills/confidence (40.7 percent), application of concepts of resilience (48.1 percent), making
progress on the fellow's plan (48.1 percent), and application of
youth development principles (44.4 percent).

Key findings

The results of this pilot study point to a number of key findings
that relate to assessing the delivery and benefit of the fellowship
and are relevant to future programming efforts. There is much
evidence that fellows benefited from the experience and showed
positive changes in key areas of knowledge, attitude, and skill.
From baseline to follow-up, they reported marked improvement in
knowing how to set goals and taking steps to achieve them, in
believing in themselves, and in involvement with groups where
they feel cared for and valued. In regard to challenges to be
addressed, the data suggest a possible disconnect for some fellows
in translating some aspects of the experience back to their work
setting. For example, in several areas, fellows recognized the
importance of strategies but reported far less effective use of the
strategy back in their work environment, such as in building relationships with youth and involving youth in decision making. One
exception to this trend is that a majority of fellows saw drawing on
the resilience perspective in planning program delivery as very
important and felt highly effective in accomplishing this. The
overall trend here may suggest areas of challenge in translating the
knowledge into practice or possibly the contextual limitations that
are placed on the fellows in their work settings.

In regard to aspects of the coaching experience, coaches highlighted the importance of fellows' being open to suggestions and

new ideas (that is, being coachable) and the value of fellows' being proactive in the coaching relationship. Coaches also identified difficulties in carving out time for coaching and making the most of the time that had been established, and they expressed concern about the plan developed by the fellows and the support that the fellows received at their work site. The areas in which coaches reported the largest fellow improvements as a result of the coaching experience were application of concepts of resilience (48.1 percent), making progress on their professional plan (48.1 percent), and application of youth development principles (44.4 percent). In addition, leadership skills and confidence was ranked as a large improvement for 40.7 percent and personal and professional balance for 26.9 percent.

Several areas of potential improvement for future programming also emerged. Themes included a belief that the residencies should focus more on translating resilience building and youth development into work experience, with consultation from coaches and peers. Specifically, the content and structure of the third residency were seen as key to facilitating this transition. Fellows expressed a need for more time and support around how to benefit from peer learning, including support in implementing the peer-to-peer strategies. They also expressed a need for coach or peer-to-peer interactions to extend beyond the six-month postresidency period because the effective translation of the residency knowledge and skills into their work site required more support over a longer period. Based on the data collected, this type of professional development can deliver tangible near-term benefits to youth service workers in regard to the effective use of resilience principles in their work.

Using the evaluation as a learning and action tool

The fellowship staff used the results of the evaluation to address several areas of delivery of the model: design of the third residency as it relates to plan design and implementation, delivery of professional support through coaching, and integration of professional networking and collaboration into the fellowship. The staff chose these three areas of focus because they were ones where the program had the resources and capacity to effect changes. Other areas would have required increased coaching time, longer fellowship, or other resources that were not available to the program.

Design of the third residency

It was clear following the third residency of the first cohort that the content and structure of this residency needed to be reexamined. The third residency focused on assisting fellows to develop a plan that they would use to apply their learning into practice. Feedback from fellows clearly indicated that significant adjustments to the original design were needed. In the initial planning, the fellowship developers did not anticipate that a large number of participants would have had little or no experience in developing or implementing plans. As the fellowship evolved, it came to include project planning strategies in the first two residencies to better prepare fellows to devise their own project plans, brainstorming what a plan might look like throughout all residency sessions, and making the process less abstract by having alumni fellows share their plans with the current fellows. The approach relied on a bottom-up planning process and strategies that helped fellows generate ideas and thoughts and then work to organize them into a coherent plan. Coaches took a larger role in supporting fellows to adjust and implement their plans, providing planning tools as needed. After making these changes, feedback was significantly more positive.

Professional support through coaching

Feedback from the evaluation led the fellowship staff to reexamine the process used to assign coaches to fellows, the clarity of how the program communicated the role of the coach to both fellows and coaches, and how the program provided support to coaches. The fellowship staff sought input from fellows about their strengths, the type of skill development they were looking for from a coach, and personality styles that they felt would contribute to the coaching relationship. Coaches were asked to explicitly share their strengths and talents with the fellowship staff. Another strategy was to have staff meet more frequently with coaching staff, share successes and challenges, engage in group problem solving, and develop additional tools to assist the coaches in supporting their own fellows.

Professional networking and collaboration

The evaluation indicated that fellows highly valued networking and collaboration with peers during the fellowship period. As time passed, fellows still valued networking and collaborations but at somewhat lower levels and found themselves to be less effective in the use of the approach. To support fellows to maintain the connections that they had developed during the fellowship and expand those connections to a larger group peers, the fellowship launched an alumni network. The purpose of the network was to strengthen the interconnections among fellows by identifying or developing opportunities for networking and professional development and to carry the message of resilience and youth development to the larger community. The network is alumni led, with support from the fellowship staff. A number of events are hosted annually for fellows that seek to provide professional development experiences for fellows, put fellows in leadership roles facilitating professional development experiences, widen individual fellows' professional networks, and enjoy one another's company during the unstructured social time that was built into these events.

Notes

1. Larson, R. W. (2000). Toward a psychology of positive youth development. *American Psychologist, 55*(1), 170–183.

2. Catalano, R. F., Hawkins, J. D., Berglund, M. L., Pollard, J. A., & Arthur, M. W. (2002). Prevention science and positive youth development:

NEW DIRECTIONS FOR YOUTH DEVELOPMENT • DOI: 10.1002/yd

Competitive or cooperative frameworks? *Journal of Adolescent Health*, *31*, 230–239; Astroth, K. A., Garza, P., & Taylor, B. (2004). Getting down to business: Defining competencies for entry-level youth workers. In P. Garza, L. M. Borden, & K. A. Astroth (Eds.), *Professional Development for Youth Workers.* New Directions for Youth Development, no. 104, 25–37.

3. Johnson, E., Rothstein, F., & Gajdosik, J. (2004). The intermediary role in youth worker professional development: Successes and challenges. In P. Garza, L. M. Borden, & K. A. Astroth (Eds.), *Professional Development for Youth Workers.* New Directions for Youth Development, no. 104, 51–64; Peake, K., Gaffney, S., & Surko, M. (2006, November). Capacity-building for youth workers through community-based partnerships. *Journal of Public Health Management Practice*, S65–S71.

4. Ashcraft, R. F. (2000). Where youth work preparation meets higher education: Perspectives from an American Humanics campus program. *Applied Developmental Sciences*, *4*, 38–46; Borden, L. M., Craig, D. L., & Villarruel, F. A. (2004). Professionalizing youth development: The role of higher education. In P. Garza, L. M. Borden, & K. A. Astroth (Eds.), *Professional Development for Youth Workers.* New Directions for Youth Development, no. 104, 75–85; Bowie, L., & Bronte-Tinkew, J. (2006). *The importance of professional development for youth workers.* Washington, DC: Child Trends; Quinn, J. (2004). Professional development in the youth development field: Issues, trends, opportunities, and challenges. In P. Garza, L. M. Borden, & K. A. Astroth (Eds.), *Professional Development for Youth Workers.* New Directions for Youth Development, no. 104, pp. 13–24.

5. Hahn, A. B., & Raley, G. A. (1998). Youth development: On the path toward professionalization. *Nonprofit Management and Leadership*, *8*(4), 387–401. Huebner, A. J., Walker, J. A., & McFarland, M. (2003). Staff development for the youth development professional: A critical framework for understanding the work. *Youth and Society*, *35*(2), 204–225.

6. Halpern, R., Barker, G., & Mollard, W. (2000). Youth programs as alternate spaces to be: A study of neighborhood youth programs in Chicago's West Town. *Youth and Society*, *31*(4), 469–506; Walker, K. C., & Larson, R. W. (2006). Dilemmas of youth work: Balancing the professional and personal. In D. A. Blyth & J. A. Walker (Eds.), *Rethinking Programs for Youth in the Middle Years.* New Directions for Youth Development, no. 112, pp. 109–118.

7. Fischer, R. L., & Craven, M. A. G. (2007, June). *Evaluation of the Treu-Mart Youth Development Fellowship Program: Results for Cohort 3.* Cleveland, OH: Mandel Center for Nonprofit Organizations, Case Western Reserve University.

ROBERT L. FISCHER *is research associate professor at the Mandel School of Applied Social Sciences at Case Western Reserve University, a faculty member at the Mandel Center for Nonprofit Organizations, and codirector of the Center on Urban Poverty and Community Development.*

MONICA A. G. CRAVEN *is executive director of the Habitat for Humanity affiliate in Youngstown, Ohio. At the time of the research she was a graduate student at the Mandel Center for Nonprofit Organizations at Case Western Reserve University.*

PATRICIA HEILBRON *is the director of the Treu-Mart Youth Development Fellowship Program at the Mandel Center for Nonprofit Organizations, Case Western Reserve University.*

How first-generation students learn to navigate education systems: A case study of First Graduate

Ben Kirshner, Manuel Gerardo Saldivar, Rita Tracy

Abstract

Students from underrepresented groups who seek to become the first in their family to attend college confront economically and racially stratified education systems. This article reports findings from an evaluation of First Graduate, an organization that offers college advising, mentoring, tutoring, and case management to first-generation students starting in seventh grade. We highlight three systems that youth say they encountered on their pathway to college: open enrollment, course taking, and college admissions. We describe how youth navigated these systems and the roles that adults played in support. Our conclusion discusses implications for how after-school programs can support first-generation students.

POSTSECONDARY EDUCATION IS critical for participation in our information-based, global economy. Completion of college predicts a number of indicators of well-being, including economic self-sufficiency, civic engagement, and educational attainment for one's children.[1] For students of color seeking to be the first in their families to attend college, however, college is often a distant goal, for reasons ranging from low-performing schools, to tracking, to skyrocketing costs of higher education.[2]

After-school programs can facilitate college access for first-generation students by helping them learn how to navigate complex and often opaque education systems. In this article, we report

NEW DIRECTIONS FOR YOUTH DEVELOPMENT, SUPPLEMENT 2011 © WILEY PERIODICALS, INC.
Published online in Wiley Online Library (wileyonlinelibrary.com) • DOI: 10.1002/yd.421

findings from an evaluation of an after-school youth program, First Graduate (FG), whose aim is to help students become the first in their families to graduate from college. We report youth participants' descriptions of three systems that they needed to navigate to get to college: school district open enrollment, high school course taking, and college admissions. In addition, we report what youth said about the key supports provided by family members and First Graduate staff members.

College access

Two principal factors help to explain low rates of college entrance and retention among first-generation students. Structural explanations point to inequalities in the kinds of resources available to students in high-poverty schools, such as qualified teachers or college-prep courses.[3] Researchers in California found that African American and Latino students were far more likely to attend schools that lack fundamental learning conditions than their white and Asian peers.[4] Moreover, rates of college eligibility for underrepresented minorities (URMs) varied dramatically across high schools. For example, in San Francisco, where FG is located, rates of college eligibility among URM high school graduates varied from a low of 8 percent at one school to a high of 73 percent at another.[5] In addition to these structural factors, an emerging consensus among researchers highlights the powerful role of cultural capital.[6] Theories of cultural capital, drawing on Pierre Bourdieu, attend to the varied ways that school bureaucracies and unwritten norms reward those fluent in cultural practices of the white middle class.[7] For example, in her book *Unequal Childhoods*, Lareau found that middle-class families were more familiar with institutional norms and more likely to advocate for their children in meetings with school personnel.[8]

From this perspective, the ability to succeed in school is as much about using cultural capital to navigate academic systems as it is about knowing calculus or deconstructing Faulkner.

As Stanton-Salazar wrote, "Success within schools . . . has never been simply a matter of learning and competently performing technical skills; rather, and more fundamentally, it has been a matter of learning how to decode the system."[9] For example, the statistics cited showing within-district disparities in San Francisco underscore how important it is that families understand the district's open enrollment system that allows students to opt out of neighborhood schools. Those families with knowledge of the open enrollment system and tendency to advocate for their children's interests are the ones who benefit in such a system. For the purposes of this article, therefore, we operationalize *cultural capital* in terms of knowledge about institutional systems and the ability to act on behalf of one's self- or family-interests within those systems. (We distinguish this institutional repertoire from other types of valuable cultural capital that are common in non-dominant communities, such as bilingualism, social networks, or political activism.[10])

The role of after-school programs

The shift in the after-school programming field toward positive youth development has led to a welcome emphasis on the skills that young people need in order to thrive rather than merely avoid problem behaviors.[11] Researchers have made great gains in identifying features of high quality, engaging programs.[12] Existing frameworks articulate important youth development outcomes, ranging from academic achievement to civic engagement.[13] Global frameworks, however, rarely address the specific experiences or needs of subpopulations, such as first-generation students. For example, few studies focus on the roles that after-school programs can play to promote the ability of first-generation students to navigate complex educational systems. Although conventional youth development competencies are critical for positive development, we propose that more attention be paid to competencies that enable first-generation students to maximize their educational opportunity in unequal educational systems. We organize this article in terms of two research questions:

- What educational systems did youth participants report learning to navigate?
- What kinds of support to navigate these systems did youth say they received from First Graduate staff and family members?

Method

First Graduate is a private nonprofit organization located in San Francisco, California, and is funded through a combination of grants and private donations. Its mission is to "help students finish high school and become the first in their families to graduate from college" (http://www.firstgraduate.org). Selected through a competitive application process during seventh grade, FG participants are admitted on the basis of evidence of their desire to succeed, their ability to benefit from the program, and the support of their parents or guardians. Each year FG recruits a new cohort of roughly twenty-four students. The program supports students through high school and college by providing mentoring, tutoring, case management, and enrichment activities. During the years when these data were collected (2006–2008), the participants had been recruited from two middle schools that served low-income neighborhoods and were populated by more than 95 percent students of color. The population of FG participants at the time was roughly 67 percent Latino, 15 percent African American, 15 percent Asian and Pacific Islander, and 3 percent European American.

Data collection and analysis

This article draws on qualitative data collected for a mixed-methods program evaluation directed by one of the authors of the article (Ben Kirshner). Analysis is based primarily on seven focus groups (n = 31) and eighteen interviews (n = 12) carried out during the 2006–2007 and 2007–2008 academic years with youth participants. Using semistructured protocols, we asked questions about these youths' experiences in school and FG and their future goals. We also draw on two focus groups with parents and interviews with staff members. Interviews and focus groups were audiotaped and transcribed.

Data analysis

These data were analyzed over several iterations using an inductive method intended to build theory.[14] First, we read transcripts in an open-ended manner, looking for themes across texts. Second, we developed a coding system intended to capture what students said about educational systems they had experienced.[15] The three of us coded the same four interview transcripts in order to achieve agreement about the meaning of codes. This process took several meetings and prompted discussion not just about technical decision rules but also the validity of constructs. After gaining shared understanding of constructs, we split up transcripts and coded them using Weft QDA, a software program. This activity generated coding bins with excerpts from interview and focus group transcripts, which we then reviewed for themes. One of us (Ben) shared a written memo with FG staff members to get their feedback about the validity of claims. FG staff members' perspective on the concept of cultural capital was useful for our analysis.

Findings

Youths' descriptions of navigating systems

Three types of systems stood out in participants' reports: high school choice, high school classrooms, and college admissions. We present them in that order because of their chronological sequence: students confronted the high school choice process in eighth grade, then adjusted to classroom expectations, and during high school began learning about college admissions.

High school open enrollment. During the time of this study the San Francisco Unified School District enabled families to opt out of neighborhood schools and request their top high school choices from a menu of comprehensive, magnet, and charter schools. Research on open enrollment in other contexts has found that families with greater knowledge of the bureaucracy, as well as greater confidence in advocating for their children—typically middle-class, college-educated families—are more likely to maximize their self-interest in this kind of open system.[16]

Our evaluation data show that more than 95 percent of FG participants opted out of neighborhood schools. Sixty-six percent enrolled in the three highest-ranked public schools (Lowell, Leadership, and Gateway), based on a composite score that combines success on 2007 state exit exams with college eligibility rates for underrepresented minorities, using data reported by UCLA IDEA.[17] An additional 9 percent matriculated in selective independent high schools from which they received financial aid.

FG participants overwhelmingly reported that their choice of high school had a positive influence on their college-going trajectories. They identified features of their high schools that they felt were valuable, such as small classes, high expectations, strong student-teacher relationships, and an emphasis on critical thinking. As one student put it, the decision to go to Leadership "changed so much of my high school experience. . . . I'm sure, that's a fact," such as by introducing him to new extracurricular activities and field trips outside San Francisco. Another student, who transferred to Leadership from a neighborhood high school after ninth grade, said that there was much more information about college there than at his old school. Similarly, students at Lowell valued its emphasis on academic work, high expectations, and access to internships.

FG students compared their high school choices favorably to those of peers who did not take advantage of the open enrollment system. Many reported that their friends from eighth grade did not engage in systematic decision making about their options. For example, one youth said that a friend of hers went to her neighborhood high school (with the lowest rates of college eligibility in the district) because everyone in her family did, "so she just thought she might as well go there." In a focus group, youth were asked if there were things that their friends missed out on by not being part of FG. They responded by talking about the opportunities they gained by attending strong high schools:

First youth: Like the opportunities, the high school opportunities.

Second youth: And someone to encourage them, (Yeah), because my friend, she's really smart, but she's going to go to the worst school, and I think that if she had all the help from [FG staff members], then she would have obviously considered another one.

Third youth: The support they give us for high school, it's like they really care about us going to a good high school, they really help us.

These examples illustrate the general theme that many FG participants took advantage of open enrollment to seek out targeted schools that they or their families thought would increase their chances of going to college. Students' use of open enrollment is evidence not just of gaining knowledge about how the choice system worked but also that youth and their families exercised agency in exploiting those opportunities.

Unwritten rules of high school course taking. FG participants talked about a number of strategies they used to "do school." Reminiscent of Stanton-Salazar's description of the forms of social and cultural capital required for school success, FG participants' accounts went beyond mastering subject matter content to include a variety of unwritten rules, ranging from learning each teacher's grading policies to knowing what activities and courses were important for college.[18] For example, youth described a variety of interpersonal strategies they developed to maintain good grades, such as learning how to communicate with and understand teachers' grading policies. As one student put it, "Talk to your teacher at the beginning of the semester so that you know what you're up against." Another student, after being asked what advice she would give to someone starting junior year, said, "Definitely know your teachers." She explained the importance of asking for missing assignments and what could be done to make up for missed work. Other strategies that students reported included turning in major papers before their due dates in order to get feedback from the teacher, finding out how cooperative work is graded, and taking advantage of opportunities to make up tests. In addition to efforts to get to know and advocate for themselves with teachers, students articulated the importance of participating in extracurricular activities such as community service.

A second insight about high school that students described was the importance of managing increasing levels of autonomy. They felt the key to navigating high school successfully was taking greater responsibility for themselves and keeping track of multiple commitments. One student, after being asked how he had changed over the prior year, framed his response in terms of becoming more self-reliant: "I just became more aware of what I need to do like to graduate and how to be . . . in college, like how I need to act. . . . Cause I need to be more responsible because I'm going to be more uh, dependent on myself not others."

Others talked about being more willing to make short-term sacrifices, such as spending an afternoon to complete homework rather than hanging out with friends, because they were more aware of how their decisions could affect their lives in the long term.

Another respondent, when asked how he had changed from last year to this year, articulated a new seriousness of purpose:

So I definitely have looked at things very different. I see that . . . if there's like a certain amount of work that I have to do, then I have to do it. Not because I need to earn a grade, but because I need to learn that kind of stuff to actually be someone in life, right. So whenever . . . something is put like in front of me like, say an obstacle in life . . . then I always have to find a way to like get through or like somehow like get over that. So, I think that's a way that I've changed from sophomore year to . . . junior year just because like, I like take things more seriously.

This student's increase in responsibility for learning and achievement, coupled with a strong sense of perseverance and initiative, helped him to succeed in impersonal systems.

College admissions. College admissions was the third system that FG youth emphasized. Youth appeared to gain a more differentiated understanding of how to evaluate and apply to colleges. For example, veteran youth learned the importance of writing multiple college essay drafts and not waiting until the last minute. Others described college entrance requirements, such as passing the state of California's "A through G" courses, which are required for college but not for high school graduation. One student, when asked what she had learned the prior year, recited the number of years of course work for each subject area that she would need to be eligible for college (four years of English and math, two years of a foreign language, and so on). In schools where college course work is not the default expectation, information such as this is essential to know at the beginning of ninth grade.

Another student, when asked what she had learned the prior year, described her dawning understanding that although Cs were good enough to pass her classes, they "won't be able to really help me in college. So I learned that I have to get better grades than Cs." Others noted the value of fulfilling extracurricular responsibilities, such as community service, as a way of being more appealing to college admissions offices. Finally, some seniors who had been on college field trips identified the importance of selecting a college that offered programs linked to specific career goals, such as teaching. In general, we found that the longer students remained in FG, the more detailed and nuanced their understanding of college requirements became.

Summary. Veteran youth participants reported learning about three types of systems that they saw as critical for access to college. The first was getting into high schools that would provide a supportive psychosocial climate and challenging classes. The second involved the importance of communicating with teachers and developing a strong sense of personal discipline in order to cope with the increasing autonomy of the high school years and variation in grading policies from teacher to teacher. The third system pertained to knowledge about college admissions and strategies for being a competitive applicant.

How First Graduate supported youth

Social and emotional support. Many youth participants valued the close relationships they formed with case managers at FG. Their descriptions of these relationships echo the literature on high-quality youth programs, in which young people regard adults as trustworthy and approachable figures who care about their lives beyond school.[19] One participant, when asked to describe FG staff, first described the academic support that her FG case manager provided, such as keeping her informed about deadlines for homework assignments and tests. Then she added, "It feels really kind of . . . close knit here. On the surface it's . . . about school and education and everything else. But they truly, really try to make sure that your life in general is going well." Another student valued how "nice" her case manager was, that she could "connect with her," and that "she's willing to talk to you at any time . . . about anything." One student was moved when an FG staff person attended her graduation ceremony; it was something that he "didn't expect." These connections were especially common among youth who had been in the program for more than one year.

Brokering relationships to complex systems. Just as valuable as the social and emotional support was FG's knowledge about how to decode and navigate education institutions. This theme was most powerful in students' descriptions of FG's role in high school open enrollment. FG actively guided students and their families by offering informational workshops about specific high schools and the application process. In addition to FG's role as information provider, youth talked about a variety of informal roles that FG staff played, such as giving rides to interviews at independent schools, meeting with parents to talk about options, and explaining application forms. One participant told a story about a form that she needed to submit to the school district after her family moved to a new address: "I needed the application . . . and I didn't know where to get it and no one's helping me, and I was frustrated, at that time, and then they [FG] helped me." A distinguishing feature of this assistance was its personal attention: FG staff members related to youth in a way that the students found "encouraging" (a word that came up several times in focus groups).

Discussions with parents in two focus groups supported these themes from youth interviews. Several parents spoke about the guidance they had received from FG staff about high schools in San Francisco. One parent explained that she knew she wanted her child to go to a private or charter school, but she had trouble fig-uring out which one would be best. She said:

When I came here, I talked to _____, who helped me a lot. And then when [my son] applied to all charter schools, he got in charter schools, but the problem was: I have to decide which one. . . . So yeah they helped me; they say, "You have to choose this one because it's small and . . . he's going to find more help, because they have after-school programs." . . . So I like it when they tell me it's a good school, and so I tell him, "Forget about the other ones; you have to go to_____."

In addition to the high school choice process, youth and their parents described learning valuable lessons about college admis-sions from FG staff. FG established a regular advisory class for participants where they learned about courses required for college and took practice entrance examinations. A trip to the FG building reveals numerous reminders of a college-going atmosphere, such as a giant map of the United States with pins marking the location of hundreds of colleges and computers that are each labeled with the name of a different university. Many students described learn-ing about colleges through FG-sponsored field trips, where they learned not just about the social atmosphere but also about specific preprofessional programs that related to their career interests.

Working in concert with families. FG engaged parents by meeting with them and developing ongoing relationships. A parent advisory group met regularly to advise staff members on programmatic decisions and plan events for families. FG case managers communicated with parents when they were concerned about a participant's behavior or attendance.

This effort to work collaboratively with parents built on a base of parental support for the FG mission. This support was critical for many newcomers to FG in seventh or eighth grade, who in some focus groups expressed the feeling that attendance requirements of after-school activities were onerous. Youth who expressed ambivalence about the program said that they remained involved with FG because their families told them to. As one student said, "They're always back, in back of me, pushing me and stuff to succeed, achieve." Another student said:

I kind of don't want to go to college but like, it's like my grandpa's dream. . . . He was the one that pushed me like to go to school and everything and then, um, my mom keeps telling me to do it. So like, I don't want to sound like I'm just doing it for them but like, I'm doing it more for them than I'm doing it for more than for myself, cause, um, I want people to be proud of me.

Another young person talked about an uncle who had provided inspiration by telling him, before he passed away, "I want you to do good and be somebody someday."

Although participants credited family members for their motivation, many also said that family members did not have detailed knowledge about the college admissions process, in part because they had not been through it themselves. In lieu of this, however, parents provided monitoring, discipline, and a focus on the future. This theme counters stereotypes that low-income families do not encourage future goals and hold low academic expectations for their children.[20] Second, it underscores that motivated first-generation students with strong support from their families also benefit from explicit guidance in the hidden or opaque rules related to college access.

Implications

The generalizability of these findings is limited because of the self-selected population of academically ambitious youth who participated in FG. Furthermore, the sample in this study does not include individuals who dropped out of FG. Despite these limitations, findings from this study point to two valuable implications for after-school practice.

Decoding systems as a developmental task

Our data show that the rules of education bureaucracies, such as the district's open enrollment system or California's college eligibility rules, were initially unfamiliar or opaque to first-generation students and their families. Youth reported that learning these rules was critical to their pathway toward college. This study contributes to recent work by Reed Larson showing that the ability to exercise agency in complex, often stratified education systems is an important developmental task for young people.[21] In addition to mastering the academic content required for postsecondary success, students need to learn how such systems work and gain confidence to advocate for themselves in those systems. We encourage after-school programs to include this kind of systems knowledge in their objectives for youths' learning and development.

Brokering as a collaborative process

Educational brokering refers to a process in which a person or organization helps to bridge cultural or linguistic differences between two parties.[22] Our data suggest that FG sometimes played a brokering role between youths' families and educational systems, such as high school open enrollment. Consistent with Cooper et al.'s findings, parents attested to the value of this brokering role as they sought to make a good life for their children.[23]

In recommending brokering as a role for after-school programs, we underscore the importance of doing so in a culturally responsive way. By *culturally responsive*, we mean that programs leverage the expertise and strengths of families, such as FG's work with the parental advisory group. Sometimes youth programs, motivated by their missions to help youth who are experiencing structural disadvantage, assume responsibility for advocacy or decision making in ways that may unintentionally exclude families. Our data suggest that parents played an essential role in providing a long-term motivational context for their children, even if they delegated responsibility for systems knowledge to FG.

Brokering should also be developmental, in that it begins with intervention and support but fades over time. When students gain admission to college, they will need to be strategic and resourceful in finding their way in a new and complex system. Research that charts the learning progression for young people's knowledge of educational systems, from relying on active assistance to developing strategies to navigate them, is an important next area of inquiry.

Notes

1. Swail, W., Cabrera, A., & Lee, C. (2004). *Latino youth and the pathway to college* (pp. 1–56). Washington, DC: Pew Hispanic Research.

2. American Youth Policy Forum. (n.d.). *Postsecondary access and success: Issue brief*. Washington, DC. Retrieved from http://www.aypf.org/programs/briefs /PostsecondaryAccessandSuccess.htm; Bedsworth, W., Colby, S., & Doctor, J. (2006). *Reclaiming the American dream* (pp. 1–33). San Francisco, CA: Bridgespan Group. Retrieved from http://www.bridgespan.org/kno_articles _americandream.htm; Jones, M., Yonezawa, S., Ballesteros, E., & Mehan, H. (2002). Shaping pathways to higher education. *Educational Researcher*, 31(2), 3–11; Oliva, M., & Nora, A. (2004). College access and the K-16 pipeline: Connecting policy and practice for Latino student success. *Journal of Hispanic Higher Education*, 3(2), 117–124.

3. Darling-Hammond, L. (2004). Inequality and the right to learn: Access to qualified teachers in California's public schools. *Teachers College Record*, 106(10), 1936–1966.

4. UC/Accord and UCLA IDEA. (2007). *California educational opportunity report*. Los Angeles, CA: University of California All Campus Consortium on Research for Diversity and UCLA Institute for Democracy, Education, and Access.

5. UC/Accord and UCLA IDEA. (2007).

6. Carter, P. (2005). *Keepin' it real: School success beyond black and white*. New York, NY: Oxford University Press; Stanton-Salazar, R. (1997). A social capital framework for understanding the socialization of racial minority children and youths. *Harvard Educational Review*, 67(1), 1–40.

7. MacLeod, J. (1987). *Ain't no makin' it: Aspirations and attainment in a low-income neighborhood.* Boulder, CO: Westview Press; Valenzuela, A. (2005). Subtractive schooling, caring relations, and social capital in the schooling of U.S.-Mexican youth. In L. Weis & M. Fine (Eds.), *Beyond silenced voices: Class, race, and gender in United States schools* (pp. 83–94). Albany: State University of New York Press.

8. Lareau, A. (2003). *Unequal childhoods: Class, race, and family life.* Berkeley: University of California Press.

9. Stanton-Salazar, R. (1997). P. 13.

10. Yosso, T. J. (2005). Whose culture has capital? A critical race theory discussion of community cultural wealth. *Race Ethnicity and Education, 8*(1), 69. doi:10.1080/1361332052000341006

11. Eccles, J., & Gootman, J. (2002). *Community programs to promote youth development.* Washington, DC: National Academies Press.

12. Durlak, J. A., Mahoney, J. L., Bohnert, A. M., & Parente, M. E. (2010). Developing and improving after-school programs to enhance youth's personal growth and adjustment: A special issue of AJCP. *American Journal of Community Psychology, 45*(3–4), 285–293; Granger, R. C. (2008). After-school programs and academics: Implications for policy, practice, and research. *Social Policy Report, 22*(2), 1–20.

13. Connell, J. P., Gambone, M. A., & Smith, T. J. (2000). Youth development in community settings: Challenges to our field and our approach. In G. Walker & N. Jaffe (Eds.), *Youth development: Issues, challenges, and directions* (pp. 281–300). Philadelphia, PA: Private/Public Ventures; Eccles & Gootman (2002); Lerner, R., Brentano, C., Dowling, E., & Anderson, P. (2002). Positive youth development: Thriving as the basis of personhood and civil society. In G. G. Noam, R. M. Lerner, C. S. Taylor, & A. von Eye, *Pathways to Positive Development Among Diverse Youth.* New Directions for Youth Development, no. 95, 11–36.

14. Strauss, A., & Corbin, J. (1998). *Basics of qualitative research: Techniques and procedures for developing grounded theory* (2nd ed.). Thousand Oaks, CA: Sage.

15. Miles, M. B. & Huberman, A. M. (1994). *Qualitative data analysis: An expanded sourcebook* (2nd ed.). Thousand Oakes, CA: Sage.

16. Howe, K., Eisenhart, M., & Betebenner, D. (2001). School choice crucible: A case study of Boulder Valley. *Phi Delta Kappan, 83*(2), 137–146.

17. Kirshner, B. (2009). *First Graduate evaluation report: Analysis of 2008-9 qualitative and quantitative data* (Tech. Rep. No. 6). Boulder, CO: University of Colorado.

18. Stanton-Salazar. (1997).

19. Strobel, K., Kirshner, B., McLaughlin, M. W., & O'Donoghue, J. (2008). Qualities that attract urban youth to after-school settings and promote continued participation. *Teachers College Record, 110*(8), 1677–1705.

20. Ng, J. C., & Rury, J. L. (2006). Poverty and education: A critical analysis of the Ruby Payne phenomenon. *Teachers College Record.* ID Number: 12596. Retrieved from http://www.tcrecord.org.

21. Larson, R. W. (2010). *SRA presidential address: Positive development in a disorderly world*. Presentation at the biennial meeting of the Society for Research on Adolescence, Philadelphia, PA.

22. Carter. (2005); Cooper, C. R., Denner, J., & Lopez, E. M. (1999). Cultural brokers: Helping Latino children on pathways toward success. *Future of Children, 9*(2), 51–57.

23. Cooper et al. (1999).

BEN KIRSHNER *is an assistant professor of educational psychology at the University of Colorado, Boulder.*

MANUEL GERARDO SALDIVAR *is a joint Ph.D. candidate in educational psychology and cognitive science at the University of Colorado.*

RITA TRACY *is a former high school teacher and is currently a doctoral student at the University of Colorado.*

Confessions of a baseball mom: The impact of youth sports on parents' feelings and behaviors

Nancy E. Peter

Abstract

To explore parents' emotional investment in and behaviors in response to youth sports, the author conducted a mixed-methods investigation to answer four research questions: (1)How do parents feel about their children's participation in organized youth team sports? (2) Which situations trigger which feelings? (3) How do parents' feelings influence their behaviors? (4) What parental characteristics (such as personal histories or demographics) are linked to different feelings and behaviors? The research indicated that many parents' feelings are triggered by their children's sports experiences and that adults must learn how to translate these feelings into productive behaviors.

After watching our son strike out three times during a game early in his first baseball season, then come up to bat for the fourth time and get two strikes, I left the bleachers and walked quickly to the women's bathroom to calm the nausea that was overwhelming me as I sat on the stands. How had someone with as little interest in male sports as I had come to care so deeply for the outcome of a game played by seven-year-old boys? What had become of me? Evidently, the same thing that happened to the countless other parents I watched

My thanks to Brian Burke, research administrator at Thomas Jefferson University, for his assistance with this article. I would also like to thank Dr. Michael J. Nakkula, a professor in the University of Pennsylvania's Graduate School of Education, who served as my academic advisor while I conducted my research.

over the ten years of my family's involvement with the neighborhood baseball organization.

Sherri Grasmuck,
Protecting Home

I HAVE WORKED in the field of out-of-school time, afterschool, positive youth development, informal science education, museum education, and environmental education for over thirty years. When I teach other people's children, my feelings and actions are usually calm and logical. I am compassionate but firm, both sensitive and fair, and generally patient and effective.

I have been a mother half as long as I have been a practitioner and now view child care and youth development through a compound and complex lens. Parenting has been a recurring, and humbling, lesson in perspective, restraint, and faith: perspective regarding the true importance (or triviality) of a situation, restraint defined as stepping back and letting go, and faith that life's big and little bumps will not permanently scar my son. I have successfully embraced these principles while navigating preschool, elementary school, summer camp, afterschool, and interactions with other kids and families. Yet my son's involvement in organized youth sports blindsided me in terms of the strength and spectrum of my emotions. The intensity of these feelings stunned me as a parent, awed me as a practitioner, and inspired me as a researcher. I hope that this study, and its results, help illuminate the issue for all three audiences.

2005 AA Championship Game

In June 2005, our son participated in his first Little League championship game. He was seven and a half years old and already a skilled and competitive player. His team had completed a great season, and the children were confident that they would win this final game. It was a beautiful spring day, and the bleachers were filled with parents, siblings, grandparents, friends, neighbors, and random baseball fans.

Despite this idyllic setting, I became more and more agitated as the game progressed. I was nervous when our son was up to bat or in catching distance of a fly ball, exhilarated when he hit the ball or made the catch, and miserable when he made a mistake of any kind. Earlier in the season, I had begun to notice the first signs of sports parent anxiety, such as elation when his team won a game and profound sadness when they lost. I recognized that my feelings often seemed disproportionately intense for a children's sports game, yet I knew that other parents shared my emotional involvement and relative extremes.

About midway through the championship game, I remember getting a drink of water, taking a deep breath, and returning to the bleachers. At that point our team was in the field, and our son was in the pitcher's position (in AA, the division for seven- and eight-year-olds, the pitcher does not actually pitch but stands by and lends moral support to the pitching machine).[1] I do not remember what happened next other than that the other team got a hit and the ball made it back to our son's glove. He paused, saw one player sliding into third and another sliding into home, and threw the ball to the catcher. The catcher missed, and the other team scored one or two runs.

Immediately our coach ran in from the outfield and yelled at our son for making a poor decision at a critical juncture. Everyone became quiet as our son stopped, looked at his glove, and began to cry. The umpire halted the game as our son walked over to my husband, who hugged and consoled him. The coach also approached our son, got down on one knee, and apologized profusely and sincerely. He told him that they would not have made it to the championship if it had not been for him. Our son stopped crying, went back out to the mound, and the game continued (our team lost that year but won the championship the following spring).

Our son got over the incident within a few hours, but my husband and I did not. During the play, I experienced outrage, embarrassment, indignation, a primal sense of maternal protection, and many other over-the-top emotions. I also knew I was reliving feelings from my own childhood—from incidents in which I felt inferior, humiliated, stranded, and scared. Over the next several days, my husband and I revisited the event many times, and I have often thought about it over the past four years. It was a remarkably painful experience for a first-time sports mom.

Although these feelings continued to gnaw at me, they did not result in any overt or antisocial behaviors. I did not yell at the coach, fight with the umpire, pull our son out of the game, battle with another parent, or indulge in any of the counterproductive parent demonstrations we so often read about or observe. My husband and I did speak with the coach privately soon after the game, and that was a cathartic rather than combustive conversation. Yet recognizing the strength of my feelings helped me understand why some parents do succumb to immediate and outrageous behaviors.

Our family has lived through many games, seasons, teams, sports, fantastic plays, and critical mistakes since the 2005 AA championship game. But it was that single event that first illuminated my dramatic attachment to our son's sports experiences. Since then I have, more than once, experienced anger at and embarrassment for adults; anger at and embarrassment for our son; intense sadness when our son's team has lost an important game and intense happiness when his team has won an important game; and a variety of equally diverse emotions. I have not always been able to diffuse my feelings, control my behaviors, or successfully sort through any of them. But I do understand that there is more here than meets the eye: how I respond to our son's participation in team sports is exaggerated by his own reactions to events, my devotion to and relationship with him, my personal wiring, my unique childhood experiences, whether my mother is sitting nearby, and any number of other trivial and important situational factors. Moreover, as I speak with other baseball, football, basketball, and hockey parents, I understand that many have similar emotional responses to their children's sports experiences. Several have witnessed or indulged in even more spectacular parental behaviors.

My own short-term solution has been to pause: if I sense that my emotions are disproportionate to a sports situation (such as outrage when a coach corrects my son), I pause before doing anything about them (such as yelling at the coach). My professional approach, however, is to further investigate the phenomenon of parental investment in organized youth team sports, how those feelings often culminate in extreme on- and off-the-field behaviors, and how this information can contribute to the field of youth sports.

Research study

To explore parents' emotional investment in and behaviors in response to youth sports activities, I conducted a mixed-methods investigation: personal reflections and experiences, a literature review, a parent survey, individual parent interviews, and field observations. Although many children live in households in which one or both parents are absent, I chose to focus on parents rather than on guardians, simply because there is little literature or research pertaining to the involvement or influence of the latter. This study combined general information about organized youth team sports (OYTS) with parental involvement in and perceptions of our neighborhood Little League specifically. This local focus is because I have access to these parents and events yet cannot generalize certain observations or findings to the field of youth sports overall.

Although the literature review provides broad background information, this research study does not attempt to thoroughly explore the benefits of children's participation in team sports, how children feel about team sports, why parents feel or behave the way they do, how parents should feel or behave, or the implications of parents' behaviors. Rather, it attempts to answer these four research questions:

1. How do parents feel about their children's participation in organized youth team sports in general and our neighborhood Little League specifically?
2. Which situations trigger which feelings?
3. How do parents' feelings influence their behaviors?
4. What parental characteristics, such as personal histories or demographics, are linked to different feelings and behaviors?

As a result of this study, I hope to provide the field with insight into parental involvement in and behaviors during organized youth sports. I would like to help program leaders better understand parents' feelings and behaviors and, as a result, develop guidelines and resources that offer ongoing suggestions and support for families. As a result of this study, I hope that some parents will reflect more openly and honestly on their feelings and actions and subsequently find optimal ways to support their children. And I hope to shed some light on my own roles, feelings, and behaviors as a sports mom, all of which will give me more to think about while I am pausing.

Organized youth team sports

Many adults remember their childhood sports participation as "walking out the back door, grabbing a baseball or hockey stick, and heading out to the street or to a nearby field to find some other kids to play with."[2] Children often had informal games that may have been similar to those of kids in other areas but with slightly different names or rules.[3] Over the past fifty to sixty years, much of this spontaneous play has been replaced by youth team sports that are organized programs supervised by adults. Although precise numbers are hard to verify, studies indicate that between 40 and 50 million school-age children currently participate in organized youth sports. Coakley attributes this growth in organized youth sports to a variety of factors:[4]

NEW DIRECTIONS FOR YOUTH DEVELOPMENT • DOI: 10.1002/yd

- Increasing numbers of single-parent families and families in which both parents work outside the home—circumstances that often necessitate structured supervision for unattended children
- The growing opinion that parents are primarily responsible for controlling and socializing their children, that child development is shaped by parenting strategies, and that sports participation provides positive character-building experiences
- The perception of professional sports activities as important cultural events, athletes as societal heroes, and youth sports as portals to scholarships and careers

Today's organized baseball, basketball, hockey, soccer, football, lacrosse, and other sports activities can cultivate a variety of short-term and long-term benefits in children.[5] Some of the best documented are:

- Learning fundamental motor skills, such as running, jumping, and hopping, and sport-specific skills, such as how to putt a golf ball or shoot a jump shot in a basket
- Learning sports-specific motor skills that can be transferred to other sports and leisure activities, promoting increased participation and involvement
- Appreciating fitness, getting exercise, and staying in shape
- Developing a sense of belonging, participating in social interactions, and enjoying peer interaction through both teammates and healthy competition
- Experiencing increased growth and maturation, self-concept and self-worth, social competence, and moral development

From my experience, several additional youth development attributes can be added to the list: patience (while waiting for one's turn or to be put into play), teamwork (giving the ball to the best-positioned player rather than making the play oneself), generosity (letting a less confident player make an important play), resilience (making a mistake and continuing with the game), self-control (staying calm when a coach or umpire makes an error), and graciousness (being respectful and polite at all times).

Our family's involvement in and benefits from youth sports both reinforce and somewhat deviate from the formal research. By the time he was five years old, our son had demonstrated that he had a passion and aptitude for physical activities, as well as the competitive nature that made him a natural for team sports. We began at the local YMCA and since that time, he has played organized baseball, soccer, floor hockey, ice hockey, flag football, regular football, and basketball. Our primary motivation has been to engage him in activities that exercise his physical skills and social-emotional development; our son's motivation has been to play baseball and have fun with his growing circle of friends. He has been exposed to, exercised, and actualized most (if not all) of the attributes listed above.

Parental involvement in organized youth team sports

Parents and other family members can have a significantly positive impact on their children's experiences with organized sports. They can alert children to sports opportunities, pay the registration fees, purchase the equipment, transport them to and from games and practices, schedule other activities around sports activities, participate in fundraisers and other volunteer activities, and manage a multitude of logistical and financial details. Parents often demonstrate appreciation for a good play and provide support and empathy when things do not go well. They can motivate children to do their best and reinforce resilience, teamwork, and all of the attributes listed above. Parents and other adults can also model sportsmanship by playing by the rules and treating others with respect.[6] In summary, child development and socialization research strongly suggests that parents play the largest role in influencing the healthy development of their children.[7]

Yet parents' emotional investment in OYTS can trigger extreme adult behaviors. Research studies, reports from the media, and testimonials from individual parents and coaches document the increasing incidence of "Little League parent syndrome," named for those adults who get so wrapped up in their children's play that they yell and scream verbal abuse and, occasionally, get physically abusive."[8] Common triggers include parents' perceptions of unfair plays, bad calls, overly critical coaches, and other injustices. Abuse can also be directed at their own children's imperfect performances. Beyond differences among the specific triggers, sports played, levels of competition, and ages of the participants, the message is alarmingly consistent: a growing number of parents at youth sports events seem to be out of control.[9] According to an Indianapolis survey of five hundred sports parents, 55 percent of the respondents said they had witnessed other parents verbally abusing youth at sporting events, and 21 percent said they had witnessed physical altercations between parents. Seventy-three percent believed verbally or physically abusive parents should be banned from future events, 22 percent would allow aggressive parents to remain in the stands, and 5 percent were unsure what to do about parents who are prone to "sports-induced tantrums."[10] Little League parent syndrome is found not only among adults who are sports nuts or prone to extreme behaviors. Parents who are normally polite, in-control people can scream from the stands, verbally abuse children and other adults, and demonstrate high levels of inappropriate activity.[11]

"Good" feelings can also trigger not-so-good behaviors. For example, many enthusiastic parents engage in behaviors that do not always model empathy or respect: they clap and cheer when players from the other team strike out, walk a batter, or miss a fly ball. I remember the Little League World Series Championship game two summers ago when the American team hit a home run in overtime. The twelve-year-old Japanese pitcher fell to the mound sobbing while thousands of Americans cheered wildly from the stands. It is one thing to verbally abuse professional sports heroes; it is another thing to humiliate a young child.

There are less public and more subtle ways in which parents' investment in youth sports can translate into counterproductive behaviors. One example is conversations with children after the game during which parents overemphasize mistakes, winning, competition, performance, and aptitude.[12] Parents may also react strongly to seemingly benign circumstances, such as when or against which team a playoff game is scheduled—overly intense reactions that may foster additional stress in children.

Extreme parental behavior can be spurred by many of the emotions I recognized during our son's 2005 Little League championship game, such as instinctively protecting one's offspring or reactivating childhood feelings of embarrassment, frustration, or failure. In addition, some parents' "adult thirst for experiencing what they watch on television" can spur disproportionately high degrees of drama.[13] Think about how you (or others) whoop, holler, pray, and curse during professional ball games; then imagine your child on the field, and add levels of love, protection, advocacy, and investment to the emotional mix.

Although there is limited research on why some sports parents behave the way they do, many authors have articulated the damage that inappropriate parental behaviors can cause. This damage includes contradicting and therefore neutralizing many of the youth development attributes that stem from sports participation, such as teamwork, patience, and graciousness. Moreover, it can turn a fun experience into one characterized by discomfort, embarrassment, and rage, thus diminishing the chances that a youngster will remain involved in the sport. When the parental display is directed at the child, such as when a parent becomes visibly angry at a poor play, the child is even more likely to abandon the sport altogether.[14] In one New Jersey study, 50 percent of the youth respondents reported that while their parents say, "Go out and have fun," they really mean, "Go out and be a star."[15] Additional counterproductive results include confusion (Why does the child have to listen to the coach but the parent does not?) and alienation (feeling at odds with rather than part of the team or sports community).

NEW DIRECTIONS FOR YOUTH DEVELOPMENT • DOI: 10.1002/yd

Fortunately, research demonstrates that parenting skills can be taught and that these skills can help parents avoid specific inappropriate practices.[16] An increasing number of efforts are targeted at educating parents and helping them to temper their extreme behaviors. Some of these strategies are simply guidelines for parental behaviors, introduced at the onset and reinforced throughout the sports season. The 2003 Massachusetts Sport Parent Code of Conduct includes rules such as, "I will remember that children participate to have fun and that the game is for youth, not adults"; "I (and my guests) will not engage in any kind of unsportsmanlike conduct with any official, coach, player, or parent such as booing and taunting; refusing to shake hands; or using profane language or gestures"; "I will never ridicule or yell at my child or other participant for making a mistake or losing a competition"; and "I will respect the officials and their authority during games and will never question, discuss, or confront coaches at the game field, and will take time to speak with coaches at an agreed upon time and place."[17] Other efforts articulate the reasons rather than rules for appropriate behavior. The "Guidelines for Supportive Parents," produced by Rutgers University, offer insights such as, "Supportive parents emphasize improved performance rather than competitive ranking"; "Supportive parents believe the sport's primary value is the opportunity for self-development"; and "Supportive parents understand and respect the differences between parental roles and coaching roles."[18]

Although some efforts are managed by the sports teams themselves, others are offered as self-help activities. "Youth Sports Parents" (http://youthsportsparents.blogspot.com/) is a blog that describes itself as "a forum to discuss the myriad ways in which adults struggle to find their place in youth sports." Youth Sports Psychology (http://www.youthsportspsychology.com/youth_sports_psychology_blog/) features an entire section entitled "The Ultimate Sports Parent." And books such as Joel Fish's *101 Ways to Be a Terrific Sports Parent* help parents understand the consequences of and reasons to moderate their behaviors.[19]

Our neighborhood Little League: A case study

Founded in 1985, our neighborhood Little League primarily serves families in the northwestern section of Philadelphia, Pennsylvania. Similar to the neighborhood in which it is located, its players come from high-income, middle-income, and low-income families; are white, African American, Latino, Asian, mixed race, and of other racial backgrounds; can be boys or girls; and represent a variety of household configurations and levels of education. Registration begins in January, and by opening day in April, over four hundred children are ready to play T-ball (ages five and six), AA (ages seven and eight), AAA (ages nine and ten), Majors (ages eleven and twelve), and Seniors (ages thirteen to sixteen). The regular season runs from the second week in April through the end of June. Traveling teams replace the in-house leagues over the summer and compete in additional games throughout the Delaware Valley.

Parents and volunteers play a vital role in our neighborhood league. A board of directors oversees registration, grounds, fundraising, parent communication, public relations, and other essential services. League commissioners manage coaches and assistant coaches, and parent volunteers help with field maintenance, fundraising activities, the concession stand, and similar functions. The broader community is also involved, from sponsoring teams and events to promoting the league in local newspapers and businesses.

Our Little League atmosphere is extremely social, congenial, and comfortable. Many families know one another and interact in other sports leagues, churches and synagogues, work environments, schools, day care and after-school programs, and local neighborhoods. As players continue in the league from year to year, parents' and children's relationships grow and add to the sense of a closely knit community. Before, during, and after games, children of all ages play together; parents and other family members visit, talk, and eat with one another; and the field often seems like one huge community picnic.

NEW DIRECTIONS FOR YOUTH DEVELOPMENT • DOI: 10.1002/yd

Our neighborhood Little League largely reflects the liberal and supportive community in which it is housed. Although there are few official rules for children's or parents' conduct, it is generally assumed that all individuals demonstrate good sportsmanship and all are treated with respect. Children and adults who do not honor this unwritten law of conduct may be subtly (a hand on the shoulder) or overtly (time out on the bench) reprimanded by others.

Our son is now participating in his sixth year of Little League (he began with T-ball in 2003). This is his first year in the Majors division. On his team are thirteen eleven- and twelve-year-old boys, although many of the Majors teams also include girls. Of all the sports in which he is involved, he enjoys baseball the most and believes it is the one he is best at. He is a very good batter and either pitches, plays first base, or is positioned in center field. He has been on four different teams and had four different coaches. His teams have won two championship games and he has been part of the Stars traveling team for four consecutive summers. Almost all of our son's closest friends also participate in the neighborhood baseball league.

Over the past six years, my husband or I have volunteered as an assistant coach, parent liaison, board member, Web site administrator, and communications coordinator. We have rarely missed a game and are often accompanied by our son's grandmother, uncle, neighborhood friends, and other fans. Many Little League families have become close friends on and off the field, and we have organized related events and picnics.

I chose this Little League as my case study because I am familiar with it, care about it, and have easy access to parents and observation opportunities. As I noted, its families represent a cross-section of races, ethnicities, household configurations, and income and education levels. Moreover, I have had many conversations with other parents regarding their baseball-related feelings and behaviors and welcomed the opportunity to explore these issues further.

NEW DIRECTIONS FOR YOUTH DEVELOPMENT • DOI: 10.1002/yd

Online parent survey

On April 26, 2009, I distributed an online survey to 579 e-mail addresses in the league's 2009 databases, representing 610 individual players. The number of addresses does not correspond with the number of players for two reasons. First, all parents and guardians are encouraged to add their e-mail addresses to the database, which means that single players may be represented by two or more addresses. Second, not all families have or provide e-mail addresses when they register.

The Youth Sports Parent Survey had been field-tested by eight parents and three research colleagues, and revised accordingly. The survey targeted current parents, explaining that participation was completely voluntary, participants' identities and answers would be kept strictly confidential, parents should complete one survey per child involved in the neighborhood Little League, parents rather than guardians should complete the survey, and participants could volunteer for individual interviews and request copies of the final report. The survey then introduced the intent, research questions, possible applications, and confidentiality assurances. Finally, it took participants through a series of questions that explored these topics:

1. Their youth sports experiences as children and as adults
2. How they and their children are currently involved in youth sports
3. Their feelings and behaviors during and after MAB games
4. Their age, gender, ethnicity, and other demographic information

The survey remained open for eleven days, during which parents received three reminders to complete the survey. On May 6, I closed the survey. At that point 153 individuals had begun the survey, 122 had completed the required questions, and 118 had made it to the last page of demographic questions.

Demographic information

Parents were asked to provide their postal code, age, race, highest level of education, annual household income, age of the child to whom the survey applied, and information about that child's siblings (see Appendix A). An average of 115 parents responded to each demographic question.

The majority of respondents (54.2 percent) lived in the neighborhood postal code (19119). The second largest population resided in an adjacent community, somewhat less affluent than the one in which the league is housed. Most parents were forty-one to fifty years old (55.9 percent), the second largest age range was thirty-one to forty years old (26.3 percent), and 10.2 percent of the parents were fifty-one to sixty years old.

The majority of respondents were either white/Caucasian (60.3 percent) or African American (34.5 percent). Most parents held a master's degree (34.8 percent), a four-year college degree (30.4 percent), or a doctoral degree (17.9 percent). While the average annual household income ranged between less than $20,000 to over $200,000, the largest group of families earned $61,000 to $81,000 (19.3 percent), $101,000 to $120,000 (15.6 percent), or $81,000 to $100,000 (11.9 percent). The age of the child to whom the survey applied spanned ages five to fifteen; the largest group were eleven year olds (17.9 percent), nine year olds (14.5 percent), and seven year olds (12 percent).

The final two questions about siblings (number and relative interest in sports) had to be discarded, as there was mistakenly no option for parents to select "no siblings."

Multiple-choice questions

With the exception of question 7, the results in the multiple-choice questions (see Appendix B) represent the average or mean answer to each question.

Parents' sports experiences. The first set of questions asked about parents' experiences with organized sports as children and (now) as adults. These questions used a Likert scale with the options of *very low, low, average, high, very high*, and *not applicable*, and 134 parents responded to each of the two questions.

Question 2 asked parents to rate their childhood sports experiences. On a scale from 1 to 5, with 1 being *very low* and 5 being *very high*, they rated their childhood sports participation most highly (3.42), followed by their parents' emotional support (3.17), their interest as a spectator (3.16), their confidence (3.15), their skill (3.05), their active participation (3.0), and their parents' involvement (2.87).

Question 3 asked about their adult experiences with organized sports. On a scale from 1 to 5, with 1 being *very low* and 5 being *very high*, they rated their interest as a spectator most highly (3.36), followed by their confidence (3.31), their skill (3.03), their interest as a participant (3.01), and their active participation (2.63).

Children's sports experiences. The fourth question asked about their children's experiences with youth sports; 132 parents answered this question. This question also used a Likert scale with the options of *very low, low, average, high*, and *very high*. On a scale from 1–5, with 1 being *very low* and 5 being *very high*, they rated their children's interest as participants most highly (4.16), followed by their active participation (4.0), their confidence (3.73), their skill (3.62), and their interest as spectators (3.42).

Parents' youth sports goals. The fifth question asked parents to rate the importance of ten different aspects of youth sports; 132 parents also answered this question. This question used a Likert scale with the options of *very unimportant, unimportant, neutral, important*, and *very important*. On a scale from 1 to 5, with 1 being *very unimportant* and 5 being *very important*, they rated having fun as most important (4.83), followed by team building (4.81), interpersonal skills (4.76), self-confidence (4.71), physical activity (4.58), athletic skills (4.11), multiple strengths (3.95), and individual strengths and competing effectively (3.58) Being part of a winning team was rated as least important (3.09). Write-in answers included learning to win or lose gracefully; knowing that team sports are an option; mixing with kids other than school friends; staying busy; developing mental skills, compassion, leadership skills, and good sportsmanship; understanding fairness, opportunity, and a work ethic; and being part of a team.

Parents' involvement. Question 6 asked parents to describe their involvement in our neighborhood Little League; 125 parents answered this question. This question presented seven tasks and used a Likert scale with the options of *never, not often, sometimes, often,* and *always.* On a scale from 1 to 5, with 1 being *never* and 5 being *always,* they most frequently attend games (4.74), followed by transporting children to games (4.65), transporting children to and from practices (4.61), attending practices (4.18), and coaching (2.84). None of the parents answered that they never or do not often attend games. Write-in volunteer duties included serving on the board, helping with fundraising, working at the concession stand, helping with the grounds crew, serving as the parent contact and team party organizer, providing team snacks, administering first aid, keeping score, and transporting others' children to and from games.

Parent feelings. Question 7 asked parents to consider thirteen different neighborhood Little League situations and how they feel about each situation by selecting one of fourteen different feeling options; 125 parents also answered this question. Most parents feel proud when their children make successful plays or when the coaches praise their children; anxious when their children are the center of attention; happy when their team wins; and accepting when their children make an unsuccessful play, a coach criticizes their children, their children are not assigned to active positions, their children are not played as often as other children, or their team loses. Most parents feel embarrassed when parents argue with one another, unhappy when parents argue with coaches or umpires, and sad when parents argue with their children.

Parent behaviors. The final set of questions explored how parents' feelings influence their behaviors, and how they behave during our neighborhood Little League games in general. These questions used a Likert scale with the options of *never, not often, sometimes, often,* and *always.* An average of 123 parents responded to each of these questions.

NEW DIRECTIONS FOR YOUTH DEVELOPMENT • DOI: 10.1002/yd

Question 8 asked parents how often they demonstrate various behaviors during our neighborhood Little League games. On a scale from 1 to 5, with 1 being *never* and 5 being *always*, they most frequently cheer for their team (4.75), followed by thanking a coach (4.17), cheering for the other team (3.41), hugging their children (3.20), thanking an umpire (3.13), crying out of happiness (1.67), arguing with their children (1.33), arguing with an umpire (1.15), crying out of unhappiness (1.12), arguing with a coach (1.09), arguing with another parent or come onto the field uninvited (1.05), or hitting or push someone (1.02). Twelve parents responded that they never hug their child, three said they never cheer for the other team, and thirteen said they never thank an umpire. Conversely, twenty-two parents answered that they always hug their child, fifteen said they always cheer for the other team, and twenty said they always thank an umpire. Only one parent admitted to sometimes hitting or pushing another adult, and only four said that they have ever come onto the field uninvited.

Question 9 asked parents how they express strong positive feelings during our neighborhood Little League games. On a scale from 1 to 5, with 1 being *never* and 5 being *always*, they most frequently express them after the game to their children (4.17), followed by expressing them during the game to another parent (3.64), expressing them after the game to another parent (3.51), expressing them after the game to the coach (3.50), expressing them during the game to their children (3.41), or expressing them during the game to the coach (2.89). Parents are least likely to keep their positive feelings to themselves (2.30). Nineteen parents said that they never keep positive feelings to themselves, and none said that they always do.

Question 10 asked parents how they express strong negative feelings during our neighborhood Little League games. On a scale from 1 to 5, with 1 being *never* and 5 being *always*, they most frequently keep them to themselves (3.27), followed by expressing them after the game to another parent (2.34), expressing them after the game to their children or during the game to another parent (2.22), expressing them after the game to the coach (2.12), and

NEW DIRECTIONS FOR YOUTH DEVELOPMENT • DOI: 10.1002/yd

expressing them during the game to the coach (1.66). Parents are least likely to express their negative feelings during the game to their children (1.50). Seven parents said that they never keep negative feelings to themselves, and three said that they always do.

Essay questions

The survey concluded with three essay questions, preceding the demographic section (see Appendix C):

1. "Describe one neighborhood Little League situation in which you experienced positive feelings such as happiness, excitement, exhilaration, or pride" (question 11). One hundred one parents responded to this question. All of the answers fell into the following six categories (some fell into more than one):
   - Their child did something positive (thirty answers): Hitting the ball for the first time, catching a fly ball, playing a position for the first time and did well, or participating in a championship game
   - Teamwork and cooperation (nineteen answers): Improving as a team, playing well in the field, rallying toward the end of a game, or shaking the other team's hands at the end of a game
   - The overall experience (nineteen answers): Watching the kids have fun, seeing all the happy children, socializing with neighbors, eating cheeseburgers, enjoying the awards ceremony, or appreciating the racial and cultural diversity
   - Their child's team won (fifteen answers): Mostly championship games or games in which the team won despite being the underdog
   - Another child succeeded (fourteen answers): Mostly in reference to children with less skill or experience catching or hitting the ball for the first time or a child simply making a good play
   - A coach's behavior (seven answers): Encouraging, hard working, praises the children, or supports kids on the opposing team

2. "Describe one neighborhood Little League situation in which you experienced negative feelings such as unhappiness, anger, embarrassment, frustration, or sadness (question 12). One hundred parents answered this question, and almost all responses fell into the following seven categories (again, some fell into more than one category):

- Coaches' behavior (thirty-four answers): Predominantly coaches who are hard on their players but also are too competitive, argue with the umpires, are overly critical of their own children, favor their own children (assign them to better positions), cannot manage their team's behaviors, do not honor their time commitment to the team, are overly concerned with winning, or model poor sportsmanship.

- None (twenty-one answers): Many parents had never had a negative experience associated with our neighborhood Little League.

- Parents' behavior (twenty answers): Are overly critical of their children, put too much pressure on their children, hit their children, argue with umpires, argue with one another, cheer when opposing players make mistakes, or coach their children from the bleachers.

- Child makes an error (thirteen answers): Sadness when a child makes a mistake, walks runners, is hard on himself or herself, cries, or otherwise breaks down; and frustration when a child makes an error because he or she is not paying attention.

- Umpires (nine answers): Bad calls, inconsistent calls, inaccurate calls, and lazy umpires.

- League administration (six answers): Late parent communication and uniform distribution, inappropriate comments from neighborhood Little League administrators during games, imbalanced rosters, and inconsistent adherence to rules.

- Children's behavior (two answers): Too much taunting and teasing when the other team's pitcher is on the mound.

3. "Describe one neighborhood Little League situation in which you were not happy with the way you behaved" (question 13).

Ninety parents responded to this final essay question. Most answers fell into one of [5] categories:

- None (65 answers): Most parents could not recall a time when they we unhappy with their behavior in a neighborhood Little League situation.
- Behavior toward children (thirteen answers): Being too critical of one's own child, publicly critiquing other members of the team, or "cheering too loudly" when members of the opposing team made a mistake.
- Behavior toward coaches (five answers): Publicly expressing anger toward another team's coach, who was perceived as being too competitive or overbearing.
- Behavior toward umpires (two answers): Questioning a call or complaining about another team's coach.
- Being overly emotional (two answers): Yelling too loudly from the stands or getting too invested in winning during a championship game.

Relating childhood experiences to adult feelings and behaviors

Brian Burke is a graduate student at Jefferson University and a neighborhood Little League assistant coach. Brian volunteered to help with my study and spent a significant amount of time studying data and creating charts and graphs. In addition, he was interested in examining the relationship between parents' involvement in sports as children and their adult feelings and behaviors. He created six discrete groups of parents: those who rated their childhood active participation, skill, and confidence as high or very high and those who rated their childhood active participation, skill, and confidence as low or very low (see Appendix D). Brian then plotted feelings and behavior data for the six groups of parents, or how the six groups each responded to questions 9 and 10. The result was that there was no visible relationship between the "high" and "low" groups and their feelings or behaviors; no patterns emerged to suggest that parents from one group have distinctly different feelings or behaviors from another. For example, high-confidence parents reported that they express their positive feelings during a game as often as low-confidence parents do; high-participation and low-participation parents hug their children, cheer for their team, and thank their coaches with equal frequency.

Parent interviews

Through the online Youth Sports Parent Survey, seventeen parents indicated that they would like to participate in individual interviews. I contacted each of these parents three times and ultimately conducted five phone and five in-person interviews. Interviews lasted between thirty and sixty minutes, with an average interview time of forty to forty-five minutes. The interviewees represented a variety of years involved in neighborhood Little League and ages of child participants and, to a lesser extent, genders and races (see Table 1). I asked each individual to respond to ten questions specific to the neighborhood league, noting that their identities and answers would be kept confidential and that they need not answer each question:

Table 1. Interview participants

Parent gender	2 women
	8 men
Parent race	9 Caucasians
	1 African American
Age of child	four 7-year-olds
	two 8-year-olds
	one 11-year-old
	two 12-year-olds
	one 15-year-old
Number of years adult has been involved in the neighborhood Little League	3 parents for 2 years
	2 parents for 3 years
	1 parent for 4 years
	1 parent for 5 years
	2 parents for 6 years
	1 parent for 8 years
Leadership roles	5 coaches
	2 assistant coaches
	3 non-coaches

NEW DIRECTIONS FOR YOUTH DEVELOPMENT • DOI: 10.1002/yd

1. "Can you tell me about the times when you felt very good at a neighborhood Little League game?" All of the parents responded that they felt good when they saw children getting along, playing as a team, displaying good sportsmanship, "watching each other's backs," or demonstrating other types of cooperative behavior. Two parents enjoyed seeing less experienced players improve, and two parents shared that they were happy when their own children hit a home run or won a championship game. Five parents specifically noted adult behaviors that made them happy: hard-working parents, coaches who supported or deliberately played less skilled players, and umpires who periodically forgave children for technical mistakes, such as not touching a base. Four parents spoke highly of a feeling of community, and one mentioned how much fun it was for children to check daily scores and standings on the league Web site.

2. "Can you tell me about the times when you did not feel good at a neighborhood Little League game?" Nine of the ten interviewees cited coaches' behavior as something that they did not feel good about: a coach who said that their own child and a player on the opposite team were not hitters; coaches who were too competitive and seemed to cultivate competitive teams; coaches who did not show up consistently; coaches who were mean to or hard on their players; aggressive coaches; coaches who argued with or "rode" the umpires; coaches who did not seem to understand positive youth development; and coaches who could not manage their parents (such as keeping them out of the dugout). One parent did not like parents who were nasty to their children, and another commented on the drunken behavior of parents from a different league. One parent complained about children from another team who chanted and taunted their pitcher.

3. "Can you tell me about times, at a neighborhood Little League game, you behaved in ways that you were not happy with?" Four of the parents I interviewed could not think of times when they behaved in ways that made them unhappy.

NEW DIRECTIONS FOR YOUTH DEVELOPMENT • DOI: 10.1002/yd

Of the other six, three yelled at an umpire over what they thought was a bad call and one argued with a coach during a game. One scolded a child for making a mistake (accidentally tripping another child), and another regretted not standing up to coaches or other parents they thought were acting inappropriately.

4. "Can you tell me about times, at a neighborhood Little League game, other adults behaved in ways that you were not happy with?" Many of these responses were similar to the replies to question 2. Five parents specified coach behaviors that made them unhappy, including not managing children who teased those on other teams, screaming at their own team members, not teaching children the right way to play baseball, and favoring their own children (on their own teams). One parent said another coach was not "generous" because he would not lend another team baseballs for a practice; another said a coach incited (engaged in hostile dialogue with) the parents from the opposite team. Four parents were unhappy with other parents who yelled mean things to players on opposite teams, criticized other children on their children's teams, and did not respect parent boundaries. One parent commented, "This is our liberal community. This is a community that stands for tolerance and respect for others. The baseball league that shares its name should reflect those values also."

5. "Have your feelings about the neighborhood Little League shifted over time? If so, how? Can you put your finger on what caused the changes?" Four parents said that their feelings about our neighborhood Little League had not changed over time (three of these had been involved for less than three years). Five of the other parents said their feelings had become more positive: the coaches are getting better, they had more appreciation for the work people put into the league, and they felt more ownership. One parent said he "recognized other parents' behaviors sooner," and another had become more competitive.

6. "Why do you think parents have strong feelings about youth sports? What are some of the things that you think trigger these feelings?" One parent did not know why some parents have such strong feelings about youth sports. The rest offered several theories. One suggested that given the amount of time parents commit to youth sports, they are bound to feel invested. Three said that parents want their children to succeed, want their children to feel good, do not want their children to fail, are afraid of how their children will be affected by failure, or want to protect them from failure. One added that parents want "fairness" for their children, and especially want other adults to be fair to their children. Two parents speculated that parents' own childhood participation in sports might make adults more emotionally involved, and two referenced parents' "vicarious participation" and "living out their dreams." Two parents spoke of public parenting—that some parents might associate their children's performance with who they are as parents, while others may be seeing their children perform in public for the first time. Finally, two parents referenced society's emotional attachment to organized sports in general: that we are trained to be highly invested in and express strong feelings during sporting events.

7. "How much do you talk with other parents about their feelings or their involvement? Do you find other parents feel similarly or different from you? How?" Three interviewees said they did not talk much about their feelings with other parents, and one did so only in extreme situations, such as when a player was hit by a ball and the parents "bonded." The other six spoke with other parents fairly often. Most said that their feelings tended to be similar. However, one parent noted that the diversity of the Little League families meant that different parents felt differently about many of the same situations.

8. "If you could change one thing about your actions in relation to your involvement in our neighborhood Little League what would it be? Anything else?" Three of the parents said they had nothing to add in terms of changing their actions. The

other parents would like to stay more positive, attend more games, work with the team more during the preseason, work better with their individual children, and "keep my mouth shut."

9. "Knowing that parents sometimes have strong feelings related to our Little League baseball, can you suggest ways in which our neighborhood Little League could better support parents? How can the league best use the information from this research project?" Responses to this question generally fell into two categories: suggestions for the league and suggestions for coaches and coaching. Five parents recommended revising league policies, such as establishing and enforcing parent and player codes of contact; instituting rules about how coaches must treat players and how players must treat one another; adding more substance to the preseason parent orientation, including what to expect and how to behave; and providing more formal opportunities for parent feedback. Five parents suggested that better coaches would result in more satisfied, less excitable parents. Better coaches would know more about baseball, teach technical skills, effectively manage parents, and work well with children. Suggestions for procuring better coaches included recruiting from a wider pool and insisting on more strenuous training. Finally, one parent added that balancing the teams better—making sure there was an even distribution of younger and older players on each team—would have a calming effect on parents.

10. "Is there anything else you would like to share regarding parents' feelings/behaviors related to youth sports or our neighborhood Little League?" Few of the interviewees had much to add by this point. A few reiterated how much they liked our neighborhood league and how lucky the community was to host it. One parent offered appreciatively that the league reflects the community's racial and socioeconomic diversity more accurately than most of its schools, restaurants, retail stores, places of worship, and other local institutions.

Observations

From April 11 through June 22, 2009, I observed each of the twenty-one in-house games in which our son participated, as well as four games between two other Majors teams and bits and pieces of AA and AAA games. These included regular season as well as play-off and championship games. I was particularly interested in parental themes that seemed to characterize multiple games, as well as parent behaviors that stood out as being unusual or extreme.

Game behavior

In the 2009 Majors games that I observed, I was cognizant of three distinct themes. The first was that parents seemed excited but not terribly agitated, particularly in comparison to my memories of AA and AAA. Most Majors parents (as well as friends and other relatives) consistently cheered for their children and teams; equally consistent were loud cries of encouragement such as, "Just throw it to the glove" (parent code for, "Stop walking players"); "Okay, you'll get the next one" (parent code for, "Stop missing plays"); and "Good cut!" (parent code for, "Stop striking out"). I witnessed few instances in which parents yelled at an umpire, a coach, or another adult. I did see several parents begin to yell something across the field, then visibly hold their tongues. I also noticed that parents seemed disinclined to cheer when a child from an opposing team struck out, walked a batter, or missed a play in the field. In fact, parents frequently praised players on the other team for good plays and good efforts. Finally, parents seemed relatively calm about watching their children pitch, something that was also more pronounced relative to my AA and AAA experiences. Although there were exceptions (one mother left the field each time her son was on the mound), most parents sat back and watched their children pitch without visible anxiety.

During the Majors play-off and championship games, parents appeared more agitated. They literally sat closer to the edge of

NEW DIRECTIONS FOR YOUTH DEVELOPMENT • DOI: 10.1002/yd

their seats and chattered less. A few parents announced, perhaps a bit too loudly, how their teams or their children were likely to win a game. Yet overall, these adults seemed relatively calm and congenial.

Parental restraint was not as evident during the AA and AAA games that I watched; this group of parents yelled at adults more frequently and showed less support for the opposing team. During one AA game, I saw a parent jump up in the bleachers and yell at the umpire, something I did not witness in any of the Majors games that I observed this year.

The second theme that emerged was what I call "dugout etiquette." There were several Majors games in which parents asked coaches, players, and other parents to quiet the players in the opposing team's dugout. This happened most often when pitchers were winding up or throwing the ball, but there were also instances in which too much noise or chanting clearly irritated other players and other adults. During one game, a parent from the other team walked over to our bleachers and asked us to help quiet down our dugout. This was followed by a conversation, among our own team's parents, about what is appropriate, inappropriate, inevitable, and unacceptable dugout behavior—a conversation that did not end in unilateral agreement.

Finally, I noted uncomfortable, sometimes public, and sometimes very loud interactions between six sets of dad coaches and their sons. Sometimes the fathers scolded their children for missing a play or not paying attention; the disapproval ranged from head shakes to gesturing, pointing, and yelling. I also witnessed dads reprimanding their sons for making mistakes as a result of inattention or fooling around. The most dramatic episodes, however, were when boys (never girls) would strike out, get tagged out, or believe that an umpire's call was unjust. This frustration often resulted in tears, throwing a bat, throwing a helmet, or stomping into the dugout, and this was when the most extreme parental behaviors occurred. I saw dads pull their sons out of the dugout, bench them for one or more innings, and, on several occasions, threaten to send them home immediately. It is important to add that I also saw each of these six dads publicly cheer, congratulate, praise, and hug their children on other occasions.

Nongame behavior

Some parental behaviors manifested themselves off the field and between games. In particular, I was privy to many, many long e-mails among MAB administrators, coaches, and parents. These e-mails ranged from a sentence or two to several lengthy paragraphs, from the topic of field maintenance to community norms and values, and from cheerful playfulness to uninhibited rage. Although I had not intended to monitor e-mail correspondence among parents, it struck me as a contemporary medium in which parents can express their sports-related feelings to multiple parties, in great detail, at any time of the day or night, and with few immediate consequences.

Research limitations

This study contains several limitations. The first, and perhaps most significant, is that the survey and interviews gathered self-reported information. As Mark Hyman states in *Until It Hurts*, "As grownups, we talk a good game about what we expect from youth sports for ourselves and for our children. If our kids make friends, have fun, and pick up a few basic skills for their sport, it's been a good season for them and for us. The reality is often more complicated."[20] Parents' descriptions of their children's experiences, their own experiences, and their feelings and behaviors may be exaggerated in some instances (such as most reporting that they *always* attend games) and minimized in others (such as the majority saying that they *never* argue with others during games).

A second limitation is that the parents who completed the online survey and volunteered for interviews were those who had access to or were comfortable with computers. Therefore, these two research activities, and the data they gathered, do not necessarily reflect the full demographic portrait of our Little League families. A third liability is that the data were collected at a single point in time: toward the beginning of one baseball season. Parents' feelings and behaviors may change significantly toward the middle or end of the season, during play-off and championship games, or at other points throughout the baseball season. And a fourth is that information gathered from a neighborhood baseball league may be interesting but cannot be generalized to other neighborhoods, cities, states, or sports.

Finally, I gathered many more data than I have time or inclination to analyze. I did explore the relationship between parents' childhood experiences and their adult feelings and behaviors. However, many more correlations could be examined: racial, gender, or age-related differences in feelings and behaviors; relationships between children's skill and confidence and parents' attitudes; thorough portraits of parents who have strong positive or negative feelings; and similar investigations.

Discussion

The combination of a literature review, the online survey, the observations and interviews, and my own feelings and reflections yielded rich and thought-provoking findings.

Family snapshots

Much of the survey provided snapshots of the families and children: their demographic information, the parents' feelings and experiences as children and as adults, and their children's level of involvement. The racial, gender, age, and socioeconomic diversity of the respondents, as well as the broad age range of their children, indicated a reasonable and informative cross-section of our Little League population. The reliance on an Internet-dependent survey and interview solicitation did remove some families from the pool. However, 610 players were represented by 579 e-mail addresses, and 231 of those 610 registered online this year. Therefore computer and Internet access may not in fact have eliminated a significant number of families from the survey sample.

Feelings about children

Not surprisingly, most parents' positive feelings were triggered by children's positive experiences. When the survey asked respondents to describe a neighborhood Little League situation in which they experienced positive feelings, the majority recounted times when their own children did something successful or felt good about themselves. The survey, interview answers, and observations confirmed that parents also felt happy when other children succeeded, particularly those who had been struggling in some way. The support for and delight in other people's children applied equally to children on other teams and on their own team. Parents also spoke highly of teamwork, cooperation, children supporting one another, and other positive group dynamics.

Many parents also described or demonstrated negative feelings associated with children's experiences, predominantly when players made errors and seemed obviously distressed or hard on themselves. Parents reported feeling anxious when their own children were the center of attention while batting, pitching, or otherwise in the spotlight. Children who demonstrated frustration, were visibly upset, cried, or "went to pieces" also triggered a great deal of sadness in respondents. These feelings of sadness and empathy seemed evenly distributed among parents' own children, children on their team, and children on other teams. Some parents, but not many, were annoyed when children from other teams taunted or seemed otherwise insensitive to their own players.

Feelings about adults

The survey and interviews indicated that parents' primary sources of negative feelings were coaches: coaches who were too competitive, were hard on their players and their own children, were hard on the respondents' children, argued with umpires, and seemed overly invested in winning or winning at all costs. Parents were also critical of coaches who did not interact well with children, could not manage disruptive parents, did not know enough about baseball, and did not attend games or practices on a regular basis. At the same time, many parents praised coaches who showed compassion for and patience with players, and who gave so much of their free time to our neighborhood Little League.

Most parents indicated that they felt good about other parents, particularly in the context of community, camaraderie, and friendship. A few indicated that they were not happy with parents who argued with coaches or umpires, were overly hard on their children, coached from the bleachers, or were insensitive to children on other teams.

Feelings about our neighborhood Little League

Many parents expressed or, through my observations, demonstrated a great deal of appreciation for our neighborhood league. Respondents continually described positive feelings triggered by community spirit, racial and socioeconomic diversity, tolerance, respect for others, socializing with other families, cooperation, being outdoors with neighbors, and other situational assets. Several parents specifically referenced how the league reflected the values, diversity, cohesion, and harmony of our community.

A few parents articulated the opposite feeling: that the level of competition or competitive nature of some coaches contradicted the cooperative and supportive nature of the community in which the league is housed. Some parents also criticized the organization for not communicating effectively with parents or inconsistently enforcing rules and official procedures.

Parent behaviors

Again, it is important to recognize that the survey and interviews reflected self-reported feelings and behaviors. According to most parents, they rarely did anything at a neighborhood Little League game that they regretted, often shared positive feelings but kept negative feelings to themselves, frequently cheered for both teams, regularly thanked coaches and umpires, and almost never came onto the field uninvited or hit or pushed anyone (only one person reported having ever hit or pushed). Although my observations did not completely verify these findings, I certainly witnessed a great deal of cheering, hugging, playfulness, and generally positive and supportive behaviors. I did observe more negative verbal outbursts and adult disagreements than the parents themselves reported, but the positive behaviors clearly outnumbered the negative ones.

Conclusions

What do parents want and expect?

The parents I surveyed and interviewed were clear about what was essential to them in terms of their children's Little League involvement: having fun was most important, and being part of a winning team was least important. It is therefore not surprising that seeing children succeed and feel good about themselves, experiencing supportive coaches, and spending time in a congenial community made most parents very happy. Conversely, frustrated children, competitive coaches, antagonistic parents, and any situation that was the antithesis of camaraderie and support was predictably unpalatable.

Why do parents feel what they feel?

This research did not explore the depth and breadth of reasons behind why parents feel passionately about youth sports. A more detailed study would investigate correlations between parents' feelings and individual demographics, childhood experiences, sports histories, and adult values. Yet the project did suggest that many factors contribute to adults' emotional attachment to children's sports experiences. We did not identify a significant link between adults' sports participation as children and their emotional investment as parents. I believe this is because so many factors, triggers, or circumstances contribute to parents' heightened responses: experiencing their children's pure happiness when they succeed; suffering their sadness when they do not succeed; taking pride in their public acclaim; nervously watching them perform in public; hoping that they do not fail; fearing that they will not handle failure well; hoping that they will not feel embarrassed; hoping that they will not embarrass themselves; wanting them to experience the instant gratification of playing well or winning; not wanting to live through their "character-building" defeat; resenting other adults who mistreat them; resenting the injustices they will invariably encounter; watching the team win and remembering what it was like to win as a children; watching the team lose and remembering what it was like to lose as a child; remembering how it felt when the Phillies won the World Series; and remembering how it felt when the Eagles lost the Superbowl. Some parents are very calm about all this (one survey respondent said, "It's Little League; it's not that deep"). And some children are much more resilient, less emotional, more relaxed, less competitive, and less invested than others, which makes a big difference in the parent-child dynamics. But for many parents, watching their children participate in youth sports triggers an unexpected avalanche of emotions that springs from a variety of obvious, subtle, past, and present sources.

Why do parents behave how they behave?

After reviewing the survey, the parent interviews, and my multiple observations, I have concluded that parents must learn how to translate their positive and negative feelings into productive behaviors. For some, this may come naturally, but for many it does not. I was struck by the suggestion, from a parent interview, that parents may be seeing their children perform in public for the first time. I was surprised to observe that parents of older players seemed more restrained than those of younger ones. One could argue that older children are more resilient and therefore ignite less anxiety in their parents. However, the level of competition, investment, and subsequent stress often increases each season, thereby mitigating the growing maturity factor. I have therefore determined that having their children participate in youth sports is a new and highly charged circumstance for many adults. Some parents must learn, through experience, not to coach from the bleachers, argue with an umpire, console or reprimand a child in the middle of a play, cheer loudly when other teams err, or contribute to their children's anxiety with visible stress of their own. Books and magazines prepare adults for infant care, toddler care, sending their children off to elementary school, introducing overnight camp, and other family milestones. Yet I have come across few resources designed to prepare parents for watching their children come up to bat; pitch one, two, three, or four innings; play in the infield or outfield; or experience both exhilaration and defeat within a two-hour time frame. It is one thing to distribute rules about appropriate and inappropriate conduct; it is another to help parents anticipate, understand, and manage their feelings and behaviors.

Recommendations

Suggestions for Our Little League

My primary recommendation for our neighborhood Little League is to empathize with and support parents as they navigate the world of youth sports. I believe our parents want, deserve, and would appreciate guidance from the organization. The parents in my study suggested that in addition to T-shirt distribution and fundraising information, parent orientations include resources and conversations about upcoming feelings and suggested behaviors. Our league could develop an official code of parent conduct, as many leagues do, explaining why these behaviors are important, as well as what will happen to those who do not comply. The league could provide ongoing support to parents such as access to other parents, an online bulletin board, or an official parent liaison. The Little League Web site could post checklists, articles, links to Web sites, and other resources that highlight parents' youth sports emotions and appropriate behaviors.

Many of the parents in my study critiqued how our league recruits, trains, and supervises its coaches. Some felt that

NEW DIRECTIONS FOR YOUTH DEVELOPMENT • DOI: 10.1002/yd

better-trained coaches who can successfully work with adults as well as children would result in better-managed parents. Others thought that it was the league's responsibility to educate and monitor its parents. I believe both can be implemented and be successful. While the league makes efforts to support its parents, it can also work specifically with coaches on issues relating to parents' feelings, behaviors, guidelines, expectations, and similar topics. Our volunteer coaches already give a tremendous amount of time, energy, and passion to the league, but the organization may be able to push them a bit further.

Finally, I suggest that our neighborhood Little League spend time exploring parents' goals for their children's participation, integrating these goals while designing and implementing the program, and referring parents and coaches back to these goals throughout the season.

Suggestions for the field

I began this article referencing my transition from practitioner to parent. Becoming a mom cultivated compassion toward other moms. Becoming a baseball mom elicited personal and professional empathy for other sports parents. Based on the results of my research and building on the suggestions for our neighborhood Little League, I recommend the following for youth sports organizations (and programs that contain competitive sports):

- Approach parents with empathy rather than judgment or distain. Accept and respect that parents may experience emotions with which they have little prior experience. Ensure that program administrators, coaches, and other staff understand and embrace this empathy.
- Articulate program norms, protocols, values, and guidelines before the program begins, not while parents are misbehaving. Formalize and regularly reference these guidelines. Reward respectful behavior, and address inappropriate actions.

NEW DIRECTIONS FOR YOUTH DEVELOPMENT • DOI: 10.1002/yd

- Similar to how we anticipate children's "problem times" such as transitions, prepare for parents' problem times, such as play-off games. Make extra efforts to calm parents during those times and remind them of collective expectations.
- Provide ongoing resources, human and otherwise. Encourage parents to support one another.
- Solicit parents' input, impressions, and suggestions. Identify productive (or at least harmless) venues in which they can express their emotions before, during, or after an event.

We parents spend much time preparing our children for and supporting them during the ups and downs of youth sports. I believe we deserve some of the same preparation, compassion, and support.

Epilogue

It has been four months since I began my Little League research project, and I have experienced another season of wins, losses, fantastic catches, heartbreaking misses, line drives, strike-outs, no-run innings, hit batters, and (my personal nightmare when our son is pitching) walked-in runs. As I read over my data and conclusions and reflect on the past several months, I recognize that I am still right there among the high end of anxious and overly emotional parents. But I increasingly realize that my feelings are often disproportionate to the situations and that I am not alone in my passion. (One mother and I joke that it goes back to prehistoric times, when the first cave mom stressed out over her cave son throwing a rock to a kid with a club.) Most important, like the other parents I surveyed, interviewed, or observed, I am learning to temper my behaviors. I no longer go into the dugout to consol my miserable pitcher; I wait until after the game to have an empathetic conversation. When a coach does not play our son where or as often as I would like, we have a civilized discussion after the game, and sometimes I forget about it entirely. I cheer as loudly as ever, but I am careful not to celebrate when a child is clearly miserable over a walk or strike-out. My stomach still ties itself into knots during play-off and championship games, but I know that the feelings will pass.

And I am taking lessons from our son. Five minutes after his tournament team lost their final play-off of the summer season, he and his teammates were running the bases, hitting balls as far as they would go, throwing their gloves at one another, wrestling in the dirt, and laughing hysterically. They were happy to be eleven-year-old boys playing baseball.

Notes

1. In Little League, the levels progress from T-Ball to AA, AAA, Majors, and Seniors.
2. Fish, J. (2007). *101 ways to be a terrific sports parent*. New York, NY: Simon & Schuster. P. 1.
3. Sachs, M. L. (2000). Lighten up, parents: Psychological aspects of youth sports. *USA Today*.
4. Coakley, J. (2006). The good father: Parental expectations and youth sports. *Leisure Studies, 25*(2), 153–163.
5. Hedstrom, R., & Gould, D. (2004). *Research in youth sports: Critical issues status*. Lansing: Institute for the Study of Youth Sports, Michigan State University.
6. Gano-Overway, L. (1999). Emphasizing sportsmanship in youth sports. *Education World*. Retrieved from www.educationworld.com/a_curr/curr137.shtml.
7. Kanters, M. (2003). *Parents in youth sports: The good, the bad, and why we need them: Research update*. Ashburn, VA: National Recreation and Park Association.
8. Sachs. (2000). P. 1.
9. Kanters. (2003).
10. Morrison, G. (2003). Parent rage in youth sports: Giving the game back to our children. *Psychology of Sports*. Retrieved from http://www.preteenagerstoday.com/articles/recreationentertainment/parent-rage-in-youth-sports-1090/.
11. Fish. (2007).
12. Fish. (2007).
13. Morrison (2008). P. 1.
14. Kaplan, R. (2008, November 6). Youth sports expert urges parents: "Let them play." *New Jersey Jewish News*.
15. Kaplan. (2008). P. 1.
16. Kanters. (2003).
17. National Youth Sports Safety Foundation 2000, p. 1.

18. Feigley, D. (2008). *Guidelines for supportive parents.* New Brunswick, NJ: Rutgers University. P. 1.

19. Youth Sports Psychology. (n.d.). The ultimate sports parent [Blog]. http://www.youthsportspsychology.com/youth_sports_psychology_blog/; Fish. (2007).

20. Hyman, M. (2009). *Until it hurts: America's obsession with youth sports.* Boston, MA: Beacon Press. P. 19.

NANCY E. PETER *is director of the Out-of-School Time Resource Center in the School of Social Policy and Practice at the University of Pennsylvania.*

Appendix A: Demographics

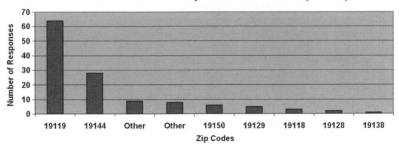

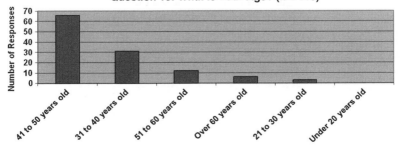

NEW DIRECTIONS FOR YOUTH DEVELOPMENT • DOI: 10.1002/yd

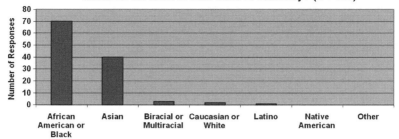

Question 16: What Is Your Race or Ethnicity? (*n* = 116)

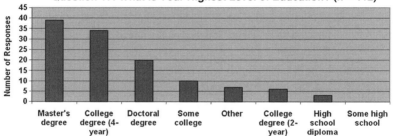

Question 17: What Is Your Highest Level of Education? (*n* = 112)

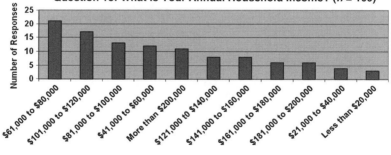

Question 18: What Is Your Annual Household Income? (*n* = 109)

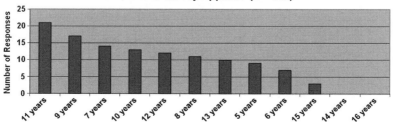

Question 19: How Old Is the Child to Whom This Survey Applies? (*n* = 117)

Appendix B: Survey Questions

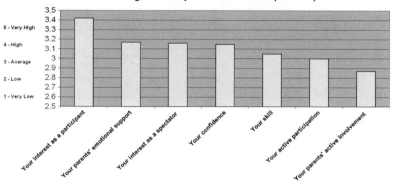

Question 2: Rate Your Experiences with Organized Sports as a CHILD (*n* = 134)

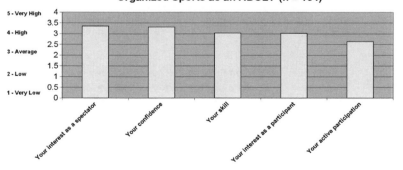

Question 3: Rate Your Experiences with Organized Sports as an ADULT (*n* = 134)

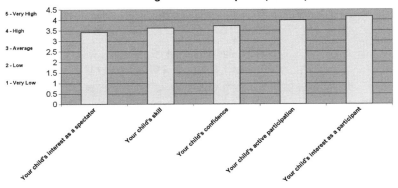

Question 4: Describe Your Child's Experiences with Organized Team Sports (*n* = 132)

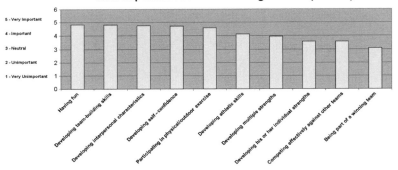

Question 5: Regarding Your Child's Participation in Youth Sports, How Important Are the Following to You? (*n* = 132)

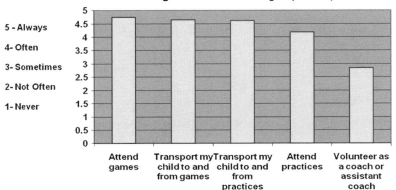

Question 6: Describe Your Involvement in the Neighborhood Little League (*n* = 130)

Question 7: Choose the Word That Best Describes How You Feel When: (n = 125)

Answer Options	Most Popular Answer	Terrific	Happy	Proud	Excited	Relieved	Accepting	Calm	Indifferent	Anxious	Frustrated	Embarrassed	Unhappy	Sad	Angry	Furious	Terrible	None of the above
Your child makes a successful play	Proud	14	30	51	25	5	0	0	0	0	0	0	0	0	0	0	0	0
The coach praises your child	Proud	9	45	54	1	3	9	0	3	0	0	0	0	0	0	0	0	1
Your child is the focus of attention	Anxious	3	15	22	23	0	3	6	10	40	0	0	0	0	0	0	0	3
Your child's team wins	Happy	7	58	9	24	2	3	2	15	0	0	0	0	0	0	0	0	5
Your child makes an unsuccessful play	Accepting	0	0	5	0	0	72	6	6	12	6	1	2	10	0	0	0	5
The coach criticizes your child	Accepting	0	0	0	0	0	56	8	4	6	6	0	14	3	8	2	0	18
Your child is not assigned to active team positions	Accepting	0	0	1	0	1	61	3	27	4	7	0	2	1	0	0	0	18
Your child is not played as often as other children	Accepting	0	0	0	0	0	40	7	11	3	24	0	13	2	2	0	0	23
Your child's team loses	Accepting	0	1	3	0	0	60	10	29	1	2	0	4	9	0	0	0	6
Parents argue with other parents	Embarrassed	0	0	0	0	0	0	2	1	4	17	35	22	8	15	7	6	8
Parents argue with the coaches	Unhappy	0	0	0	0	0	0	1	2	2	17	25	27	3	18	10	5	15
Parents argue with the umpire	Unhappy	1	0	0	0	0	0	1	11	2	12	23	24	3	17	7	7	17
Parents argue with their children	Sad	0	0	0	0	0	2	1	2	1	10	10	22	24	10	15	18	10

NEW DIRECTIONS FOR YOUTH DEVELOPMENT • DOI: 10.1002/yd

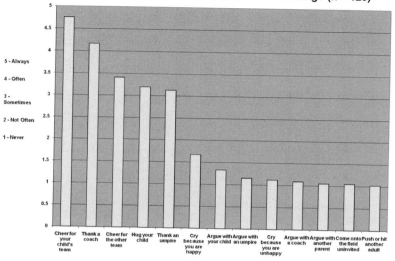

Question 8: How Often Do You Do the Following? (*n* = 123)

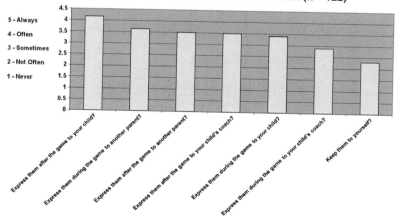

Question 9: When You Have Positive Feelings at a Little League Game, How Often Do You: (*n* = 122)

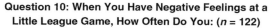

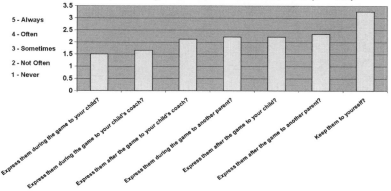

Appendix C: Essay Questions

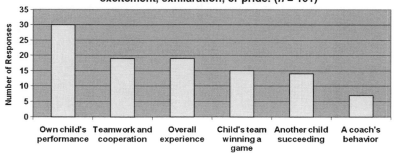

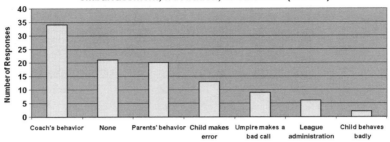

Question 12: Describe one neighborhood Little League situation in which you experienced negative feelings such as unhappiness, anger, embarrassment, frustration, or sadness: (*n* = 100)

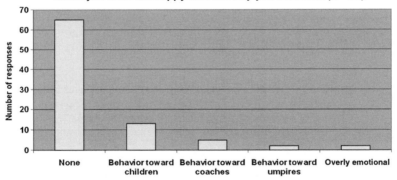

Question 13: Describe one neighborhood Little League situation in which you were not happy with the way you behaved: (*n* = 90)

NEW DIRECTIONS FOR YOUTH DEVELOPMENT • DOI: 10.1002/yd

Appendix D: Correlations

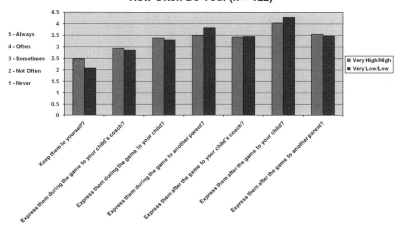

**Childhood Confidence Correlated with Question 9:
When You Have Positive Feelings at a Little League Game,
How Often Do You: (*n* = 122)**

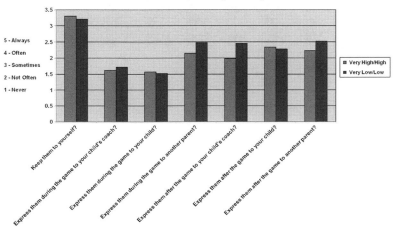

**Childhood Confidence Correlated with Question 10:
When You Have Negative Feelings at a Little League Game,
How Often Do You: (*n* = 122)**

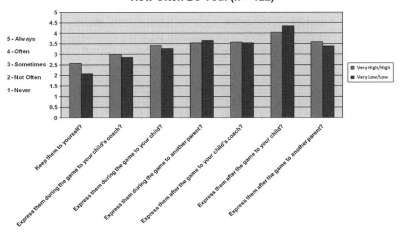

Childhood Skill Correlated with Question 9:
When You Have Positive Feelings at a Little League Game,
How Often Do You: (*n* = 122)

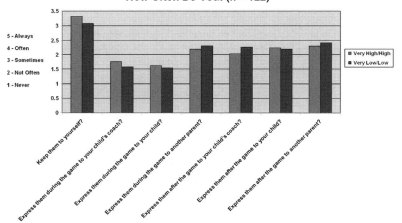

Childhood Skill Correlated with Question 10:
When You Have Negative Feelings at a Little League Game,
How Often Do You: (*n* = 122)

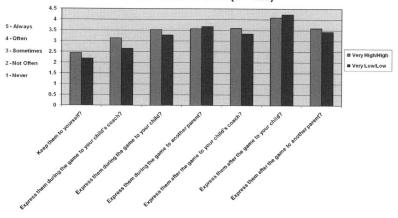

Childhood Participation Correlated with Question 9:
When You Have Positive Feelings at a Little League Game,
How Often Do You: (*n* = 122)

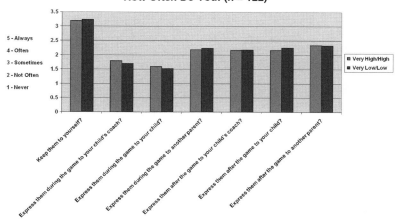

Childhood Participation Correlated with Question 10:
When You Have Negative Feelings at a Little League Game,
How Often Do You: (*n* = 122)

NEW DIRECTIONS FOR YOUTH DEVELOPMENT • DOI: 10.1002/yd